9/14

D0509190

Holiday Hats
for Babies

**CAPS, BERETS
& BEANIES
TO KNIT FOR
EVERY
OCCASION**

DEBBY WARE

The Taunton Press

NORTHERN PLAINS
PUBLIC LIBRARY
Ault, Colorado

Text © 2014 by Debbie Ware
Photographs © 2014 by Alexandra Grablewski except where noted below
Illustrations © 2014 by The Taunton Press, Inc.

All rights reserved.

The Taunton Press
Inspiration for hands-on living®

The Taunton Press, Inc., 63 South Main Street
PO Box 5506, Newtown, CT 06470-5506
e-mail: tp@taunton.com

EXECUTIVE EDITOR: SHAWNA MULLEN
ASSISTANT EDITOR: TIM STOBIERSKI
PROJECT EDITOR: ASHLEY LITTLE
COPY EDITOR: BETTY CHRISTIANSEN
INDEXER: BARBARA MORTENSON
COVER DESIGN: KIM ADIS
INTERIOR DESIGN: DEBORAH KERNER
LAYOUT: TINSLEY MORRISON
ILLUSTRATOR: CHRISTINE ERIKSON
PHOTOGRAPHERS: ALEXANDRA GRABLEWSKI EXCEPT FOR PHOTOS ON
PP. 6, 8, 9, 22, 24, 25, 48, 50, 52, 54, 55, 66, 68, 69, 74, 76, 77, 82, 84, 85, 86,
88, 89, 100, 103, 108, 110, 111, AND 116 BY JAMES RODERICK
PROP & WARDROBE STYLIST: KIM FIELD
STYLIST: NIKI DELETIS
BABY WRANGLER: SARAH SEBASTIANO

The following names/manufacturers appearing in *Holiday Hats for Babies* are trademarks:
Lion Brand® Chenille Thick & Quick®, Lion Brand® Homespun®, Lion Brand®
LB Collection® Superwash Merino, Lion Brand® Vanna's Glamour®

Library of Congress Cataloging-in-Publication Data

Ware, Debby, 1952-
  Holiday hats for babies : caps, berets & beanies to knit for every occasion / Debby Ware.
     pages cm.
  Includes index.
  ISBN 978-1-62710-102-8
  1. Knitting--Patterns. 2. Hats. 3. Caps (Headgear) 4. Infants' clothing. I. Title.
  TT825.W372845 2014
  746.43'2--dc23
                        2014020740

Printed in the United States of America
10 9 8 7 6 5 4 3 2 1

Dedication

For my mother and father,
Charlotte & Sam Milstein

Acknowledgments

I would like to thank my editor, Shawna Mullen. Her enthusiastic responses
to all my designs will always be appreciated.

Contents

Introduction

Is there a new baby on the way? There is nothing more fun or precious than creating a unique and charming token of affection for any baby in your life. These hand-knit hats will quickly become heartfelt hand-me-downs that any mother will cherish.

Small projects like hats are a joy to create because not only do they make wonderful gifts, but they also knit up very quickly. The unique hats found in *Holiday Hats for Babies* will help celebrate the special days of the year—even if it's just the arrival of fall or the first snow day of the winter.

Whether you are a beginner or an advanced knitter, *Holiday Hats for Babies* will guide you through each project with clear and easy-to-follow instructions. The yarns suggested—cottons and soft wools—are perfect for babies because they're soft and washable. You'll find a variety of designs in the collection, from traditional designs with a little twist to totally modern shapes.

Getting Started

In case you need a little help, the sections in the back of the book will explain must-have tools, knitting basics, and special stitches including duplicate stitching, bobbles, I-cord, and Pom-Poms. I've also included abbreviations and step-by-step illustrations for all knitting levels. Even the experienced knitter needs a few reminders!

The real fun in some of these hats is in the embellishment. From fuzzy Pom-Poms to glittery birthday candles, these little additions are what make some hats truly one of a kind. Read through the instructions before you start knitting, and you will have no problems with any of these fun touches. Even the easiest embellishment technique creates great results, especially when you're knitting for a baby.

Now is the time to have fun, so pick up your needles and get started creating a wide assortment of fabulous projects for the new little one!

Winter Is Wonderful

Holly Holiday Hat

This seasonal sensation with giant holly leaves and bright red berries will help any little one get into the swing of the holidays!

Sizing

Small (14-in. circumference)

Large (18-in. circumference)

Figures for larger size are given below in parentheses. Where only one set of figures appears, the directions apply to both sizes.

Yarn

DK Weight smooth yarn

The hat shown is made with S.R. Kertzer Super 10 Cotton: 100% mercerized cotton, 4.4 oz. (125 g)/ 250 yd. (228.6 m).

Yardage

50 (70) yd. Super 10 Cotton #3997 Scarlet

40 (50) yd. Super 10 Cotton #3532 Soft Yellow

60 yd. Super 10 Cotton #3764 Peppermint

Materials

16-in. U.S. size 4 circular needle

Four U.S. size 4 double-pointed needles

One pair U.S. size 4 straight needles

Stitch marker

Tapestry needle

GAUGE

22 sts = 4 in.

SEED STITCH

Rnd 1: *K1, P1; rep from * to end of rnd.

All other rnds: K the P sts and P the K sts.

Directions

HAT BASE

With circ needles and Scarlet, CO 72 (100) sts. Place a st marker on right needle and, beginning Rnd 1, join CO sts together, making sure that sts do not become twisted on needle.

Note: Always keep the unworked yarn on the WS of the work and sl sts pw.

Rnd 1: P.

Rnd 2: Drop Scarlet and attach Peppermint. With Peppermint, *K1, sl 1 wyib; rep from * to end of rnd.

Rnd 3: With Peppermint, *P1, sl 1 wyib; rep from * to end of rnd.

Rnd 4: Drop Peppermint. K entire rnd with Scarlet.

Rnd 5: P with Scarlet.

Rnds 6–13: Rep Rnds 2–5 two (3) times for a total of 3 (4) repetitions.

Cut Peppermint and work Seed st with Scarlet for 1½ (2½) in.

Cut Scarlet and attach Peppermint. K1 rnd. P1 rnd.

Cut Peppermint and attach Soft Yellow. K9 (15) rnds.

DECREASE ROUNDS

Dec Rnd 1: *K7 (8), K2tog; rep from * to end of rnd.

Dec Rnd 2: *K6 (7), K2tog; rep from * to end of rnd.

Continue in established pattern, knitting 1 less st between decs until you have approx 4–6 sts on the needle. Cut the yarn, leaving a 6-in. tail. Thread a tapestry needle and pass it through the remaining sts on the needle. Bring the tail to the WS of the work.

HOLLY LEAVES

With straight needles and Peppermint, CO 5 sts. K1 row, P1 row.

Row 1 (RS): *K1f&b, YO, K1, YO, K1, YO, K2—9 sts.

Rows 2, 4, 6, 10, 12, 16, and 18: P.

Rows 3 & 9: K4, YO, K1, YO, K4—11 sts.

Rows 5 & 11: K5, YO, K1, YO, K5—13 sts.

Row 7: BO 3 sts, K2, YO, K1, YO, K6—12 sts.

Row 8: BO 3 sts, P8—9 sts.

Row 13: BO 3 sts, K9—10 sts.

Row 14: BO 3 sts, P6—7 sts.

Row 15: Sl 1, K1, psso, K3, K2tog—5 sts.

Row 17: Sl 1, K1, psso, K1, K2tog—3 sts.

Row 18: BO all sts.

Make 6 leaves.

Sew 2 leaves together (WS facing in) to make 1 fat leaf. You will have 3 fat leaves. Carefully sew each leaf base to the top of the hat.

HOLLY BERRIES

With straight needles and Scarlet, CO 1 st. K1f&b 3 times, creating 6 sts. Turn.

Rows 1 & 3: K.

Row 2: P.

Row 4: (P2tog) 3 times (AL)—3 sts.

Row 5: K.

Row 6: P3tog. BO.

Knot CO and BO tails together to make the berry. Use the tails to attach the berries to the center of the hat.

Make 3 berries.

FINISHING

Weave in all loose ends. Thread a tapestry needle with Scarlet and use Duplicate Stitch (see p. 114) to decorate the first row of Soft Yellow at the bottom of the crown. See the photograph on the facing page for visual reference. Your Holly Holiday Hat is ready for the holidays!

Glittery Snow Cap

Welcome winter with a shimmering snowy-white hat wrapped up like a small gift. Let it shine with the help of little glittery speckles.

Sizing

One size (16- to 18-in. circumference)

Yarn

DK Weight smooth yarn

Sport Weight acrylic yarn with metallic polyester

The hat shown is made with Tahki Cotton Classic: 100% mercerized cotton, 1.75 oz. (50 g)/108 yd. (100 m) and Lion Brand® Vanna's Glamour®: 96% acrylic, 4% metallic polyester, 1.75 oz. (50 g)/202 yd. (185 m).

Yardage

80 yd. Cotton Classic #3001 White

30 yd. Vanna's Glamour #861-113 Ruby Red

40 yd. Vanna's Glamour #861-170 Topaz

40 yd. Vanna's Glamour #861-100 Diamond

Materials

16-in. U.S. size 4 circular needle

Four U.S. size 4 double-pointed needles

Stitch marker

Tapestry needle

GAUGE

22 sts = 4 in. with Vanna's Glamour

Directions

HAT BASE

With circ needle and White, CO 90 sts.

Place a st marker on right needle and, beginning Rnd 1, join CO sts together making sure that sts do not become twisted on needle.

P1 rnd. K1 rnd. P1 rnd.

K5 rnds.

Attach Topaz and Diamond.

Finger Rnd: *Using the Cable Cast-On (see p. 114) and Topaz, CO 6 sts, then BO those 6 sts. K4 sts with White. Using Diamond, CO 6 sts, then BO those 6 sts. K4 sts with White; rep from * for remainder of rnd.

With White, K5 rnds.

Rep Finger Rnd using only Diamond for all fingers and placing them between fingers of previous rnd.

K5 rnds.

Continue in established pattern, placing fingers

Continue in established dec pattern, knitting 1 less st between dec and working 6 rnds between decrease rnds. Switch to dpns when necessary until approx 40 sts rem. Cut White. Attach Ruby Red.

CROWN

Ridge Rounds

Without working any decs and with Topaz, K1 rnd. P1 rnd.

With Diamond, K1 rnd. P1 rnd.

Cut Topaz and Diamond. With Ruby Red, K2tog to end of rnd. P1 rnd.

K2tog until you have 4 sts rem on needles.

FINISHING

Work I-Cord (see p. 115) for 9 in. Cut the yarn, leaving a 6-in. tail. Using a tapestry needle, thread the tail through the remaining sts on the needle. Bring the tail down the center of the I-Cord to the WS of the crown of the hat.

With a dpn and Ruby Red, CO 4 sts and work a second I-Cord for 9 in.

Cut the yarn, leaving a 6-in. tail. Using a tapestry needle, thread the tail through the remaining sts on the needle. Bring the tail down the center of the I-Cord to hide. Attach this I-Cord to the crown of the hat and, using both I-Cords, tie a big bow on top of the hat.

between fingers of previous rnds for the even spacing of fingers and alternating between using two colors per rnd and just Diamond per rnd.

At the same time you are creating Finger Rnds, make the following dec:

After working 3 Finger Rnds and 5 rnds even, *K8, K2tog; rep from * to end of rnd.

Hanukah Hat

All nine candles on this menorah are burning brightly! Whether you're celebrating the Festival of Lights or just enjoying the sparkle, this hat is sure to add an extra spark to the holiday.

Sizing

One size (16- to 18-in. circumference)

Yarn

DK Weight smooth yarn

The hat shown is made with Lion Brand LB Collection® Superwash Merino: 100% superwash merino, 3.5 oz. (100 g)/306 yd. (280 m).

Yardage

80 yd. Superwash Merino #486-174 Spring Leaf

30 yd. Superwash Merino #486-108 Denim

30 yd. Superwash Merino #486-098 Ivory

10 yd. Superwash Merino #486-114 Cayenne

Small amount of glitter yarn

Small amount of green ribbon yarn (optional)

Materials

16-in. U.S. size 4 circular needle

Four U.S. size 4 double-pointed needles

One pair U.S. size 4 straight needles

Stitch marker

Tapestry needle

GAUGE

22 sts = 4 in.

SEED STITCH

Rnd 1: *K1, P1; rep from * to end of rnd.

All other rnds: K the P sts and P the K sts.

Directions

HAT BASE

With circ needle and Spring Leaf, CO 100 sts.
Place a st marker on right needle and, beginning Rnd 1, join CO sts together, making sure that sts do not become twisted on needle.

Rnd 1: P.

Work Seed st for 1½ in.

HAT BODY

K all sts for 10 rnds.

DECREASE ROUNDS

Dec Rnd 1: *K8, K2tog; rep from * to end of rnd.
K5 rnds.

Next dec rnd: *K7, K2tog; rep from * to end
of rnd.
K5 rnds.

Next dec rnd: *K6, K2tog; rep from * to end
of rnd.

Continue in established dec pattern, knitting 1 less
st between decs and placing sts on dpns when
necessary until you have completed the 6th
dec rnd.

CAYENNE RIDGE ROUND

Drop Spring Leaf and attach Cayenne.

Ridge Rnd 1: *With Cayenne, K.

Ridge Rnd 2: P.

Drop Cayenne and pick up Spring Leaf.

With Spring Leaf, K3 rnds, continuing with dec
rnds.*

Rep from * to * once more, then rep Ridge Rnds 1
and 2.

You will have 4–6 sts on needles. Cut the yarns,
leaving a 6-in. tail. Thread tapestry needle and
pass the yarn through the rem sts on the needle.
Secure to WS of work.

MENORAH

Candelabrum Branches

With Denim and 2 dpns, CO 4 sts and create the
following I-Cords (see p. 115) for the branches of
the Menorah:

2 I-Cords measuring 1½ in. long

2 I-Cords measuring 2 in. long

2 I-Cords measuring 3 in. long

2 I-Cords measuring 4 in. long

Center Base

With Denim and 2 dpns, CO 6 sts and work I-Cord
for 3 in.

Using the photograph as a reference, sew I-Cords
onto hat in the shape of the Menorah.

Candles

With Ivory and 2 dpns, CO 4 sts and create the
following I-Cords for the candles of the Menorah:

8 I-Cords measuring 2 in. long

1 I-Cord measuring 2½ in. long

FINISHING

Sew candles onto hat.

With glitter yarn, create small French Knots (p. 115)
on the tip of each candle for the glowing flame.

Optional: With ribbon yarn, create an elegant touch
at the base of each candle by simply using a
tapestry needle and the running stitch.

Snowy Celebration Hat

Ring in the New Year with style while wearing this sparkling hat that says it all: CELEBRATE!

Sizing

One size (16- to 18-in. circumference)

Yarn

DK Weight smooth yarn

The hat shown is made with Sirdar Bonus Baby Changes DK: 100% acrylic, 3.5 oz. (100 g)/ 361 yd. (330 m).

Yardage

100 yd. Bonus Baby Changes DK #563 Lemon Spray

Small amount of glitter yarn

Small amount of pale yellow silk yarn

Small amount of mint green acrylic yarn

Materials

One pair U.S. size 5 straight needles

Two U.S. size 5 double-pointed needles

Stitch marker

Tapestry needle

GAUGE

22 sts = 4 in.

Directions

HAT BASE

Note: The entire hat is knit in Garter st.

With Lemon Spray and straight needles, CO 160 sts.

K10 rows.

DECREASE ROWS

Make the following dec every other row, placing a marker on one end of work to help mark your dec row:

Dec row: K1, ssk, K to last 3 sts on needle, K2tog, K1.

Continue with these decs until you have approx 5 sts left on needle.

BO all sts.

FINISHING

With a tapestry needle, carefully sew sides together, leaving an approx 1-in. opening at base.

With Lemon Spray and your choice of glitter and silk yarns, CO 4 sts and create at least two 6-in. I-Cords (see p. 115) for top of hat. Leave a 6-in. yarn tail at the end of each I-Cord. Attach to top, pulling the yarn tail through the I-Cords and gathering them to create a squiggle effect.

With mint green and using a simple running stitch, embroider CELEBRATE across the middle of the hat.

Peppermint Candy Cap

Giant Pom-Poms and a swirly ridged crown make this cap perfect for your own little peppermint sweetie.

Sizing

Small (14-in. circumference)

Large (16-in. circumference)

Figures for larger size are given below in parentheses. Where only one set of figures appears, the directions apply to both sizes.

Yarn

DK Weight smooth yarn

DK Weight eyelash yarn

The hat shown is made with S.R. Kertzer Super 10 Cotton: 100% mercerized cotton, 4.4 oz. (125 g)/250 yd. (228.6 m) and Stylecraft Icicle: 62% polyester, 38% metallized polyester, 1.75 oz. (50 g)/87 yd. (80 m).

Yardage

60 (70) yd. Super 10 Cotton #3443 Shell Pink

25 yd. Super 10 Cotton #3722 Celery

10 yd. Super 10 Cotton #3997 Scarlet

40 yd. Super 10 Cotton #3475 Geranium

Small amount of Icicle #1140 Crystal

Materials

16-in. U.S. size 4 circular needle

Four U.S. size 4 double-pointed needles

Stitch marker

Tapestry needle

Pom-Pom maker (1 ½ in.)

GAUGE

22 sts = 4 in. with Super 10 Cotton

Directions

HAT BASE

With circ needles and Scarlet, CO 72 (80) sts. Place a st marker on right needle and, beginning Rnd 1, join CO sts together, making sure that sts do not become twisted on needle.

Rnd 1: P.

Rnd 2: Cut Scarlet. K entire rnd with Shell Pink.

Rnd 3: P with Shell Pink.

With Shell Pink *K1, K1f&b; rep from * to end of
   rnd—108 (120) sts.

K with Shell Pink for a total of 12 rnds.

Drop Shell Pink. Attach Celery. *K1 rnd. P1 rnd.
   Drop Celery, pick up Shell Pink, and K4 rnds;
   drop Shell Pink, pick up Celery, and rep from *
   until you have a total of 4 Celery ridges.

SWIRL TOP

Cut Shell Pink and Celery. Attach Geranium
   and start dec rnds, changing to dpns when
   necessary.

Dec Rnd 1: *K7 (8), K2tog; rep from * to end
   of rnd.

Dec Rnd 2: *K6 (7), K2tog; rep from * to end
   of rnd. Continue in established pattern, knitting
   1 less st between decs. When 4–6 sts rem,
   cut the yarn, leaving a 6-in. tail. Thread a tapestry
   needle and pass it through the remaining sts left
   on the needle. Bring the tail to the WS of the work.

Rnd 4: Drop Shell Pink. Attach Geranium and
   K entire rnd.

Rnd 5: P with Geranium.

Rep Rnds 2–5 until you have 4 ridges of Shell Pink
   and 3 ridges of Geranium. Cut Geranium, attach
   Scarlet, and K entire rnd. P next rnd. Cut Scarlet
   and pick up Shell Pink.

FINISHING

Weave in all loose ends.

Thread a tapestry needle with Geranium, pinch the
   hat at the first Celery pure rnd, and create a Welt
   (see p. 116) by sewing together the top and
   bottom pieces using even running stitches.

Using Shell Pink and Icicle, make three Pom-Poms
   (see p. 116) and attach them securely to the top
   of the hat.

Cup of Love Hat

Celebrate Mother's Day with a teacup filled with love. Be sure to have extra pink yarn on hand if you'd like to knit even more hearts to fill the cup.

Sizing

Small (16-in. circumference)

Large (18-in. circumference)

Figures for larger size are given below in parentheses. Where only one set of figures appears, the directions apply to both sizes.

Yarn

DK Weight smooth yarn

The hat shown is made with Tahki Cotton Classic: 100% mercerized cotton, 1.75 oz. (50 g)/108 yd. (100 m).

Yardage

30 (40) yd. Cream

60 (80) yd. #3446 Light Pink or #3812 Light Blue, plus 25 yd. #3446 Light Pink for hearts

30 (35) yd. #3722 Light Spring Green

Materials

16-in. U.S. size 4 circular needle

Five U.S. size 4 double-pointed needles

Stitch marker

Tapestry needle

Yarn scraps or stuffing

GAUGE

22 sts = 4 in.

Directions

HAT BASE

With circ needle and Light Spring Green, CO 90 (100) sts. Place a st marker on right needle and, beginning Rnd 1, join CO sts together, making sure that sts do not become twisted on needle.

Note: Always keep unworked yarn on the WS of your work and sl sts pw.

Rnd 1: P.

Rnd 2: Drop Light Spring Green and attach Light Pink/Light Blue. With Light Pink/Light Blue, *K1, sl 1 wyib; rep from * to end of rnd.

Rnd 3: *P1, sl 1 wyib; rep from * to end of rnd.

Rnd 4: Drop Light Pink/Light Blue and, with Light Spring Green, K entire rnd.

Rnd 5: P.

Rep Rnds 2–5 two more times, ending with a completed Rnd 5.

Cut Light Spring Green and with Light Pink/Light Blue, K every rnd until entire piece measures 4 (5) in.

Ridge Rnd: Drop Light Pink/Light Blue and attach Light Spring Green. K1 rnd. P1 rnd.

Rep Hat Base Rnds 2–5.

Cut Light Spring Green and with Light Pink/Light Blue, K8 (10) rnds.

Dec Rnd 1: *K8, K2tog; rep from * to end of rnd.

Dec Rnd 2: *K7, K2tog; rep from * to end of rnd.

Continue in established pattern, placing sts on dpns when necessary and knitting 1 less st between decs until you have approx. 4–6 sts on needles. Cut the yarn, leaving a 6-in. tail. Using a tapestry needle, thread the tail through the rem sts on the needle, then secure the tail on the WS of the work.

TEACUP

Note: This teacup is knit from the inside center bottom to the outside center bottom. The WS of the knitted work is hidden, creating the appearance of a genuine teacup.

Inside Bottom

With Cream and 1 dpn, CO 8 sts. K1f&b into each st. **At the same time,** work those sts onto 4 dpns, joining into the rnd and being careful not to twist sts.

Cont to inc 1 st with k1f&b at end of each dpn until you have 10 sts on each needle.

Cut Cream and attach Light Spring Green. K1 rnd. P1 rnd.

Cut Light Spring Green and attach Light Pink/Light Blue.

With Light Pink/Light Blue, inc 1 st at each end of each dpn every 4th rnd until 72 sts rem—18 sts on each dpn.

Drop Light Pink/Light Blue and attach Light Spring Green.

With Light Spring Green, K1 rnd. P1 rnd.

Cut Light Spring Green and attach Cream.

K3 rnds.

Dec rnds: *Drop Cream and pick up Light Pink/Light Blue. Work 1 rnd, dec 1 st at the beginning and end of each dpn as follows: ssk, K to last 2 sts on needle, K2tog. Cont with dec on all 4 needles.

Drop Light Pink/Light Blue. Pick up Cream and K3 rnds.*

Rep from * to * for a total of 4 Light Pink/Light Blue stripes, ending with 3 rnds of Cream—10 sts on each needle.

Drop Cream and attach Light Spring Green. K1 rnd, P1 rnd.

Cut Light Spring Green. With Cream, continue dec at both ends of every needle each rnd until 8 sts remain. Cut the yarn, leaving a 6-in. tail. Using a tapestry needle, thread the tail through the rem sts on the needle. Pull the yarn, gathering sts tightly together, then secure the tail to the WS of the work.

Using a tapestry needle and Light Spring Green, sew the lip of the teacup together with a small, even running stitch.

With dpns and Cream, CO 3 sts and create an I-Cord approx 3 in. long. BO. Attach to side of teacup for handle.

SAUCER

With dpn and Cream, CO 8 sts.

K1f&b into each st. Divide sts evenly onto 4 dpns, joining into the rnd and being careful not to twist sts. K1 rnd.

K1f&b into the first and the last st on each dpn until there are 20 sts on each needle. Work even for 4 rnds.

Cut Cream and attach Light Pink/Light Blue. (K1 rnd, P1 rnd) twice.

Cut Light Pink/Light Blue and attach Light Spring Green. K1 rnd. P1 rnd. K1 rnd. BO all sts.

Sew Saucer to top of hat.

Sew Teacup securely on top of Saucer.

HEART

With Light Pink and dpns, CO 4 sts.

K1f&b in every st—8 sts.

Divide 8 sts over 3 needles—4 sts on needle 1, 2 sts each on needles 2 and 3.

With 4th dpn, join to work in rnd, taking care not to twist sts.

K1 rnd.

Next inc rnd: Needle 1: K1f&b, K to last st, K1f&b.

Needle 2: K1f&b, K to end of rnd.

Needle 3: K to last st on needle, K1f&b.

Next inc rnd: K.

Rep these 2 inc rnds until there are 28 sts total on needles.

Next rnd: K2tog, K5. Join with needle 3 using a 5th dpn and K5, K2tog from needle 3. You will now work the 12 sts on the first 2 needles. The other 14 sts are held on the 2 dpns for other side of heart and will be worked later.

Next rnd: Working on one side of heart:

Needle 1: K2tog, K2, K2tog.

Needle 2: K2tog, K2, K2tog—8 sts total for this rnd.

Place both needles parallel and with WS facing, BO all sts using Three-Needle BO.

Stuff heart with a small amount of yarn scraps or stuffing before finishing 2nd side of heart.

Join yarn at center of heart to work other side of the heart with 14 remaining sts.

Next rnd: Working on opposite side of heart:

Needle 1: K5, K2tog.

Needle 2: K5, K2tog—12 sts total for this rnd.

Next rnd:

Needle 1: K2tog, K2, K2tog.

Needle 2: K2tog, K2, K2tog—8 sts total for this rnd.

Rep from * to *.

Create as many hearts as you desire to fill your cup!

FINISHING

Sew center of heart together and bring all tails to bottom point of heart to securely connect it to the inside center of the teacup.

Weave in all loose ends.

St. Pat's Hat

Everyone is Irish on this special day. Celebrate with nothing less than a giant knitted shamrock for your baby to wear proudly.

Sizing

Small (16-in. circumference)

Large (18-in. circumference)

Figures for larger size are given below in parentheses. Where only one set of figures appears, the directions apply to both sizes.

Yarn

DK Weight smooth yarn

The hat shown is made with Tahki Cotton Classic: 100% mercerized cotton, 1.75 oz. (50 g)/108 yd. (100 m).

Yardage

80 (100) yd. #3725 Deep Leaf Green

50 (60) yd. #3722 Light Spring Green

50 yd. #3726 Bright Lime Green

Materials

16-in. U.S. size 4 circular needle

Five U.S. size 4 double-pointed needles

One pair U.S. size 4 straight needles

Stitch markers

Tapestry needle

Yarn scraps or stuffing

GAUGE

22 sts = 4 in.

SEED STITCH

Rnd 1: *K1, P1; rep from * to end of rnd.

All other rnds: K the P sts and P the K sts.

Directions

HAT BASE

With circ needle and Deep Leaf Green, CO 80 (100) sts. Place a st marker on right needle and, beginning Rnd 1, join CO sts together, making sure that sts do not become twisted on needle.

Rnd 1: P.

Work in Seed st until entire piece measures 4 (5) in.

RIDGE ROW

Note: Always keep unworked yarn on the WS of your work and sl sts pw.

Drop Deep Leaf Green and attach Light Spring Green.

K1 rnd. P1 rnd.

Rnd 1: Drop Light Spring Green and pick up Deep Leaf Green. With Deep Leaf Green, *K1, sl 1 wyib; rep from * to end of rnd.

Rnd 2: With Deep Leaf Green, *P1, sl 1 wyib; rep from * to end of rnd.

Rnd 3: Cut Deep Leaf Green and K entire rnd with Light Spring Green.

Rnd 4: P.

Drop Light Spring Green and attach Bright Lime Green.

CROWN

K1 rnd with Bright Lime Green, placing a 2nd st marker after the 1st 40 (50) sts of the rnd. You now have 2 st markers on your needles.

Begin making the following dec on this and every rnd after:

Dec Rnd: *K to 2 sts before markers, ssk, K1, sl marker, K2tog.

Rep Dec Rnd 3 more times.

Cut Bright Lime Green and pick up Light Spring Green. Continue with decs as established to the crown of hat, placing sts on dpns when necessary until you have about 4–6 sts left on needle. Cut yarn, leaving a 6-in. tail. With tapestry needle, thread tail through remaining sts on needle. Secure tail on the WS of work.

SHAMROCK (MAKE 2)

With Bright Lime Green and straight needles, CO 4 sts.

Row 1 (RS): *K1f&b into each of the 1st 3 sts, K1—7 sts.

Row 2 and all even rows (WS): P.

Row 3: *K1f&b into each of the 1st 6 sts, K1— 13 sts.

Rows 5 & 7: K.

Row 9: K5, s2kp, K5—11 sts.

Row 11: K4, s2kp, K4—9 sts.

Row 13: K3, s2kp, K3—7 sts.

Row 15: K2, s2kp, K2—5 sts.

Row 16: P.

Cut yarn, leaving a 4-in. tail.

Note: Do not cut final 4th leaf. You can use that tail to attach all leaves.

Leave 5 sts on needle or place onto a holder.

Repeat rows 1–16 three more times for a total of 4 clover leaves.

Place all 4 leaves onto 1 needle.

CONNECT THE SHAMROCKS

Row 1: K4, K2tog *K3, K2tog; rep from * to last 4 sts, K4.

Row 2: P.

Row 3: K2tog entire row—8 sts.

Row 4: P.

Row 5: K2tog entire row—4 sts.

Pass 2nd, 3rd, and 4th sts over 1st st on needle. BO last st.

With tails from all leaves, connect Shamrock leaves by carefully sewing a 1-in. seam starting at the base of the leaves.

ATTACH SHAMROCK

With RS facing out, close Shamrock leaves by putting a small amount of stuffing into each clover leaf to help it stand tall on the tip of the hat.

Carefully sew Shamrock to top of hat using the entire base of the 2 bottom leaves as anchors.

STEM (MAKE 2)

With Bright Lime Green and dpns, CO 3 sts and work I-Cord (see p. 115) for about 2 in.

Attach a Stem to each side of the Shamrock at the base, letting the rest of the Stem curl up.

FINISHING

Weave in all loose ends.

Spring Has Sprung

Spring Has Sprung Hat

Capture the carefree feeling of spring. Pink rose bouquets on top will add elegance to any garden party—or just a day at the park.

Sizing

Small (16-in. circumference)

Large (18-in. circumference)

Figures for larger size are given below in parentheses. Where only one set of figures appears, the directions apply to both sizes.

Yarn

DK Weight smooth yarn

The hat shown is made with Tahki Cotton Classic: 100% mercerized cotton, 1.75 oz. (50 g)/108 yd. (100 m).

Yardage

60 (80) yd. Cotton Classic #3726 Bright Lime Green

40 yd. Cotton Classic #3446 Light Pink

20 yd. Cotton Classic #3533 Bright Yellow

30 yd. Cotton Classic #3722 Light Spring Green

10 yd. Cotton Classic #3459 Deep Hot Pink

30 (40) yd. Cotton Classic Cream

Materials

16-in. U.S. size 4 circular needle

One pair U.S. size 4 straight needles

Five U.S. size 4 double-pointed needles

Stitch marker

Tapestry needle

GAUGE

22 sts = 4 in.

Directions

HAT BASE

With circ needle and Bright Lime Green, CO 90 (110) sts. Place a st marker on right needle and, beginning Rnd 1, join CO sts together, making sure that sts do not become twisted on needle.

Rnd 1: P.

Rnd 2: *K1, P2; rep from * for entire rnd.

Continue in established Rnd 2 ribbing pattern until the entire piece measures 5 in.

Cut Bright Lime Green and attach Bright Yellow.

RIDGE ROW

With Bright Yellow K1 rnd. P1 rnd.

HAT CROWN

Cut Bright Yellow and attach Cream. K10 rnds.

DECREASE ROUNDS

Dec Rnd 1: *K8, K2tog; rep from * to end of rnd.

Dec Rnd 2: *K7, K2tog; rep from * to end of rnd.

Continue in established pattern, knitting 1 less st between decs and switching to dpns when necessary until you have approx 5 sts on the needle. Work an I-Cord (see p. 115) with the remaining 5 sts for approx 4 in. Cut the yarn, leaving a 6-in. tail. Thread a tapestry needle and pass it through the center of the I-Cord. Secure the tail on the WS of the work.

ROSES

With Light Pink and straight needles, CO 10 sts.

Row 1 (RS): K.

Row 2 & all even rows (WS): P.

Row 3: K1f&b of each st—20 sts.

Row 5: K1f&b of each st—40 sts.

Row 7: K1f&b of each st—80 sts.

Row 8: P.

BO all sts.

SMALL LEAF

With Light Spring Green and straight needles, CO 5 sts.

Row 1 (RS): K2, YO, K1, YO, K2—7 sts.

Rows 2, 4, 6, 8, 10, 12 & 14 (WS): P.

Row 3: K3, YO, K1, YO, K3—9 sts.

Row 5: K4, YO, K1, YO, K4—11 sts.

Row 7: K.

Row 9: Ssk, K to last 3 sts, K2tog, K1—9 sts.

Row 11: Ssk, K to last 3 sts, K2tog, K1—7 sts.

Row 13: Ssk, K to last 3 sts, K2tog, K1—5 sts.

Row 15: K2tog, K1, K2tog—3 sts.

BO.

WELT

Thread a tapestry needle with Deep Hot Pink, pinch the hat at the Ridge Rnd, and create a Welt (see p. 116) by sewing together the top and bottom pieces using even running sts.

FINISHING

To shape rose, twist to form spiral. Sew roses and leaves to top of hat, sewing the leaves onto the I-Cord in the center. Create a Deep Hot Pink French Knot (see p. 115) in the center of each flower.

Weave in all loose ends. Now spring has sprung!

Sherbet and Strawberries Topper

Celebrate this wonderful fruit with a spring-colored cap. A good strawberry is plump, beautifully shaped, and delicious—just like your little newborn!

Sizing

Small (14-in. circumference)

Medium (16-in. circumference)

Large (18- to 20-in. circumference)

Figures for larger sizes are given below in parentheses. Where only one set of figures appears, the directions apply to all three sizes.

Yarn

DK Weight smooth yarn

The hat shown is made with Sirdar Snuggly Tiny Tots: 90% acrylic, 10% polyester, 1.75 oz. (50 g)/150 yd. (137 m) and Tahki Cotton Classic: 100% mercerized cotton, 1.75 oz. (50 g)/108 yd. (100 m).

Yardage

40 (70, 80) yd. Tiny Tots #917 Peaches

25 (30, 40) yd. Tiny Tots #918 Lemony

10 (30, 40) yd. Tiny Tots #920 Baby Green

30 yd. Cotton Classic #3446 Light Pink

2 (3, 4) yd. pink silk rattail cord

Materials

16-in. U.S. size 5 circular needle

Four U.S. size 5 double-pointed needles

One pair U.S. size 4 straight needles

Stitch marker

Tapestry needle

GAUGE

22 sts = 4 in. with Tiny Tots and size 5 needles

DOUBLE MOSS STITCH

Rnd 1: *K2, P2; rep from * to end of rnd.

Rnd 2: K all K sts, P all P sts.

Rnd 3: P all K sts, K all P sts.

Rnd 4: Rep Rnd 3.

Directions

HAT BASE

With circ needle and Peaches, CO 70 (80, 100) sts. Place a st marker on right needle and, beginning Rnd 1, join CO sts together, making sure that sts do not become twisted on needle.

Rnd 1: P.

Work in Double Moss st until entire hat measures 3 (3½, 4) in.

Cut Peaches yarn and attach pink silk rattail cord. K1 rnd. P1 rnd.

Cut pink silk rattail cord and attach Baby Green. K8 (10, 13) rnds.

DECREASE ROUNDS

Dec Rnd 1: *K8, K2tog; rep from * to end of rnd.

Dec Rnd 2: *K7, K2tog; rep from * to end of rnd.

Continue in established pattern, knitting 1 less st between dec and placing sts on dpns when necessary, until you have approx 4–6 sts on the needles.

Work I-Cord (see p. 115) with remaining sts for approx 2 in.

Cut the yarn, leaving a 6-in. tail. Thread a tapestry needle and pass it through the remaining sts on the needle. Secure the tail on the WS of the work.

STRAWBERRIES (MAKE 3)

With Light Pink and dpns, CO 6 sts.

Rnd 1: * K1f&b, kl; rep from * to end of rnd.

Rnd 2, 4, 6, & 8: K.

Rnd 3: * K1f&b, K2; rep from * to end of rnd.

Rnd 5: * K1f&b, K3; rep from * to end of rnd.

Rnd 7: * K1f&b, K4; rep from * to end of rnd.

Rnd 9: * K1f&b, K3; rep from * to end of rnd.

Attach Baby Green.

Rnd 10: *With Baby Green, K1, with Light Pink, K4; rep from * to end of rnd.

Rnd 11: *With Baby Green, K3, with Light Pink, K2; rep from * to end of rnd.

Rnd 12: Cut Light Pink and with Baby Green, K all sts.

Rnd 13: *K2tog, K3; rep from * to end of rnd.

Rnd 14: K2tog until 4 sts rem on needles.

With the rem sts work I-Cord (see p. 115) for ½ in.

Stuff Strawberry with scrap yarn and sew up seam.

FINISHING

With RS facing and using Lemony, pick up 70 (80, 90) sts evenly around the base of the hat. Place a st marker at the beginning of the round and work Double Moss st for 1 (2, 2½) in. BO all sts.

Weave in all loose ends. Thread a tapestry needle with Baby Green and attach each Strawberry to I-Cord at top of hat.

Fold up Lemony base on the ridge where color was connected to make a brim.

April Fool's Cap

Looking for the perfect way to celebrate with your little jester? This wild and crazy hat is the perfect topper for any foolish prankster!

Sizing

Small (14-in. circumference)

Large (18-in. circumference)

Figures for larger size and alternate color choices are given below in parentheses. Where only one set of figures appears, the directions apply to all sizes.

Yarn

DK Weight smooth yarn

The hat shown is made with Tahki Cotton Classic: 100% mercerized cotton, 1.75 oz. (50 g)/108 yd. (100 m).

Yardage

30 yd. Cotton Classic #3424 Deep Red

30 yd. Cotton Classic #3459 Deep Hot Pink

30 yd. Cotton Classic #3726 Bright Lime Green

30 yd. Cotton Classic #3533 Bright Yellow

30 yd. Cotton Classic #3532 Pale Lemon Yellow

30 yd. Cotton Classic #3807 Dark Turquoise

30 yd. Cotton Classic #3401 Light Bright Orange

40 (50) yd. Cotton Classic #3932 Amethyst

30 (40) yd. Cotton Classic #3001 White

30 yd. Cotton Classic #3722 Light Spring Green

Materials

16-in. U.S. size 4 circular needle

Four U.S. size 4 double-pointed needles

Stitch marker

Tapestry needle

Small amount of polyester filling

GAUGE

22 sts = 4 in.

Directions

BASE

With circ needle and Amethyst, CO 90 (120) sts. Place a st marker on right needle and join CO sts together, making sure that sts do not become twisted on needle. Purl 1 rnd. Drop Amethyst. Attach Light Spring Green and Pale Lemon Yellow.

RIBBING BASE

Note: Always keep unworked yarn on the WS of your work and sl sts pw.

Rnd 1: With Light Spring Green, K entire rnd.

Rnd 2: P.

Rnd 3: Drop Light Spring Green. Pick up Pale Lemon Yellow and *K1, sl 1 wyib; rep from * to end of rnd.

Rnd 4: *P1, sl 1 wyib; rep from * to end of rnd.

Rnd 5: Drop Pale Lemon Yellow. With Light Spring Green, K entire rnd.

Rnd 6: P.

Rep Rnds 3–6 three more times, ending with a completed Rnd 6.

Cut Light Spring Green and Pale Lemon Yellow. Pick up Amethyst.

K1 rnd. P1 rnd.

Cut Amethyst and attach White.

K10 rnds.

Attach Light Bright Orange.

FINGERS

Finger Rnd: *Using the Cable Cast-On (p. 114), CO 6 sts, then BO 6 sts. K5 sts with White; rep from * to end of rnd.

Cut Light Bright Orange. Attach Deep Hot Pink and rep Finger Rnd one time.

Cut Deep Hot Pink and pick up White. K1 rnd.

HORNS

Horn Fronts

Cut White. Attach Dark Turquoise and K30 (40) sts, leaving 60 (80) sts live on the needles. *Turn work and P30 (40) sts. Work dec row on next and every other row until you have 3 sts left on needle. BO all sts.*

Dec row: K1, ssk, K to last 3 sts, K2tog, K1.

Attach Bright Lime Green to live sts. K30 (40) sts. Rep from * to *.

Attach Deep Red to remaining 30 (40) sts. Rep from * to *.

You have now completed the front of each horn and there are no sts on needles.

Horn Backs

Holding your work with the RS facing, bend the front of the Dark Turquoise horn down and expose the join between the hat and the Horn Front. With Light Bright Orange, pick up 30 (40) sts evenly for back of horn. Rep from * to * to complete the Dark Turquoise horn back. Rep from * to * for each rem horn, using Deep Hot Pink for the back of the Bright Lime Green horn and Bright Yellow for the back of the Deep Red horn.

Dark Turquoise Horn Sides

Folding the Dark Turquoise and Light Bright Orange triangles down as you did for the fronts and backs of the horns, pick up 20 (25) sts evenly across each side of both pieces for a total of 40 (50) sts.

Row 1 (dec): K1, K2tog, work to last 3 sts, K2tog, K1.

Row 2: P1 row.

Rep Rows 1 and 2 until 3 sts remain on needle. BO all sts.

Rep for other side of horn using Bright Yellow.

Bright Lime Green Horn Sides

Use the same instructions as for Dark Turquoise Horn Sides, using Deep Red and Bright Yellow.

Deep Red Horn Side

Use the same instructions as Dark Turquoise Horn Sides, using Dark Turquoise and Bright Lime Green.

HAT CROWN

Folding all triangles away from you and with RS facing, attach Amethyst and pick up 90 (120) sts evenly around hat. Place st marker at beginning of round and K10 rnds.

Dec rnd: *K8, K2tog; rep from * to end of rnd.

Next dec rnd: *K7, K2tog; rep from * to end of rnd.

Continue in established dec pattern, knitting 1 less st between dec and switching to dpns when necessary until 5 sts rem.

Cut the yarn, leaving a 6-in. tail. Use a tapestry needle to draw tail through the rem sts.

FINISHING

Using a tapestry needle, sew seams of each horn, being careful to leave a space to stuff with polyester filling before sewing the last seam.

With Deep Red and Bright Yellow, create 3 small Pom-Poms (see p. 116) and attach to tip of each horn.

Using a tapestry needle and White yarn, sew a running st along the base of the horns and tug slightly to help the horns stand upright.

Weave all loose ends into back of hat.

Baby Chick Cap

Here, chick, chick! A sweet, fluffy chick sitting in its own basket among the grass—what could be a more perfect hat for your little newborn?

Sizing

One size (14-in. circumference)

Yarn

DK Weight smooth yarn

DK Weight eyelash yarn

The hat shown is made with S.R. Kertzer Super 10 Cotton: 100% mercerized cotton, 4.4 oz. (125 g)/ 250 yd. (228.6 m) and Stylecraft Icicle: 62% polyester, 38% metallized polyester, 1.75 oz. (50 g)/87 yd. (80 m).

Yardage

60 yd. Super 10 Cotton #3223 Tan

30 yd. Super 10 Cotton #3841 Caribbean or #3446 Cotton Candy

25 yd. Super 10 Cotton #3722 Celery

1 yd. Super 10 Cotton #3997 Scarlet

1 yd. Super 10 Cotton Black

50 yd. Icicle #1142 Sunlight

Materials

16-in. U.S. size 4 circular needle

One pair U.S. size 4 straight needles

Stitch marker

Tapestry needle

GAUGE

22 sts = 4 in. with Super 10 Cotton

SEED STITCH

Rnd 1: *K1, P1; rep from * to end of rnd.

All other rnds: K the P sts and P the K sts.

Directions

HAT BASE

With circ needles and Tan, CO 72 sts. Place a st marker on right needle and, beginning Rnd 1, join CO sts together making sure that sts do not become twisted on needle.

Note: Always keep unworked yarn on the WS of your work and sl sts pw.

Rnd 1: P. Drop Tan and attach Caribbean/
Cotton Candy.

Rnd 2: *K1, sl 1 st with Caribbean/Cotton Candy;
rep from * to end of rnd.

Rnd 3: *P1, sl 1 st with Caribbean/Cotton Candy;
rep from * to end of rnd.

Rnd 4: Drop Caribbean/Cotton Candy and pick up
Tan. K entire rnd.

Rnd 5: P with Tan.

Rep Rnds 2–5 eight times. Cut all yarn. Attach
Celery.

GRASS

Using the Cable Cast-On (see p. 114), create
blades of grass that alternate in length from 6 sts
long to 8 sts long as follows: With Celery, *CO
6 sts, BO those 6 sts, K1, CO 8 sts, BO those
8 sts, K1. Rep from * for the entire rnd. K1 rnd
with Celery.

CHICK

Cut Celery and attach Icicle. You will divide the
work in half and work back and forth on straight
needles—not in the round—for the remainder
of the hat.

Row 1: K36 with Icicle.

Work in Seed st for 2 1/2 in. BO all sts and cut the
yarn, leaving a 10-in. tail.

Attach Icicle on RS where the work was divided for
the first half. K1 row. Work back and forth in
Seed st for 2 1/2 in.

Dec Rows: K2tog 5 times at beg of the next
2 rows.

Next Dec Rows: K2tog at the beg and end
of each row 4 times until you have 22 sts on
the needle.

Cut the yarn, leaving a 10-in. tail. Thread a tapestry
needle and pass it through the rem sts on
the needle. Pull tightly and—presto!—the head
of the chick takes shape. With the same tail,
sew a seam along the top of the chick and
secure the remainder of the yarn to the inside of
the work. With the other tail, carefully sew up the
width of the chick.

FINISHING

Weave in all loose ends. With Black, make two
French Knots (see p. 115) for the eyes of the
chick. Make a large French Knot using Scarlet for
the beak. This cute chick cap is complete!

Tea Garden Hat

Think tea parties in spring! Chenille gives a touch of elegance to this hat—perfect for Sunday brunch in the garden or playing dress-up with your little girl.

Sizing

One size (14-in. circumference)

Yarn

DK Weight smooth yarn

Bulky Weight chenille yarn

Worsted Weight ribbon yarn

The hat shown is made with S.R. Kertzer Super 10 Cotton: 100% mercerized cotton, 4.4 oz. (125 g)/250 yd. (228.6 m); Lion Brand Chenille Thick & Quick®: 91% acrylic, 9% rayon, 100 yd. (91 m); and Trendsetter Yarns Monarch: 53% nylon, 47% acrylic, 1.75 oz. (50 g)/60 yd. (55 m).

Yardage

30 yd. Super 10 Cotton #3712 Hazel

10 yd. Super 10 Cotton #3936 Wisteria

2 yd. Super 10 Cotton #3402 Nectarine

20 yd. Chenille Thick & Quick #950-178 Basil

20 yd. Monarch #10 Forest Heather

Materials

16-in. U.S. size 4 circular needle

16-in. U.S. size 9 circular needle

Four U.S. size 4 double-pointed needles

Stitch marker

Tapestry needle

GAUGE

22 sts = 4 in. with Super 10 Cotton and size 4 needle

Directions

HAT BASE

With the size 9 circ needle and Chenille, loosely cast on 60 sts. Place a st marker on right needle and, beginning Rnd 1, join CO sts together making sure sts do not become twisted on needle.

Rnd 1: P.

Rnd 2: K.

Rnd 3: P.

Rnd 4: K.

Rnd 5: P.

Cut Chenille and attach Hazel. K next rnd with the size 4 circular needle. Remember to K this first rnd tightly. After all the sts are on the size 4 circ needle, K15 rnds.

Next Rnd: Drop Hazel and attach Chenille. K next rnd, with the size 9 circular needle. P next rnd.

RIDGE ROUNDS

Drop Chenille. Attach Monarch. K next rnd, with the size 4 circ needle. P next rnd.

*Drop Monarch, pick up Hazel, and K4 rnds. Drop Hazel and pick up Monarch. K1 rnd, P1 rnd. Rep from *.

You will have 2 bands of Hazel and 3 ridges of Monarch. Cut Hazel and Monarch. Attach Wisteria and K1 rnd, putting the sts on dpns.

DECREASE ROUNDS

Dec Rnd 1: *K4, K2tog; rep from * to end of rnd.

Dec Rnd 2: *K3, K2tog; rep from * to end of rnd.

Continue in established pattern, knitting 1 less st between decs until 5–6 sts are on needle.

Cut Wisteria and attach Chenille. Loosely work I-Cord (see p. 115) for 3 rnds. BO.

FINISHING

Weave in all loose ends. Thread a tapestry needle with Wisteria and, using Duplicate Stitch (see p. 114) and the photograph on the facing page as a visual reference, embroider diagonal lines around base of hat. Use Nectarine to make French Knots (see p. 115) at the upper end of each line. With Chenille, make a small Pom-Pom (see p. 116) and attach to top of hat.

Mother's Day Bouquet Beanie

Mother's little wonder will look adorable with a wild selection of roses atop a sweet pastel cap.

Sizing

Small (16-in. circumference)

Large (19-in. circumference)

Figures for larger size are given below in parentheses. Where only one set of figures appears, the directions apply to both sizes.

Yarn

DK Weight smooth yarn

Heavy worsted chenille yarn

The hat shown is made with Tahki Cotton Classic: 100% mercerized cotton, 1.75 oz. (50 g)/ 108 yd. (100 m) and Muench Touch Me: 72% rayon microfiber, 28% wool, 1.75 oz. (50 g)/61 yd. (56 m).

Yardage

30 (35) yd. Cotton Classic Cream

70 (80) yd. Cotton Classic #3446 Light Pink

40 (50) yd. Cotton Classic #3722 Light Spring Green

30 (35) yd. Cotton Classic #3001 White

25 (30) yd. Cotton Classic #3932 Amethyst

25 yd. Cotton Classic #3532 Pale Lemon Yellow

30 yd. Touch Me #3642 Dark Pink

40 yd. Touch Me #3608 Vibrant Pink

Materials

16-in. U.S. size 4 circular needle

Five U.S. size 4 double-pointed needles

One pair U.S. size 6 straight needles

Stitch marker

Tapestry needle

GAUGE

22 sts = 4 in. with Cotton Classic and size 4 needle

Directions

HAT BASE

With circ needle and White, CO 80 (100) sts. Place
a st marker on right needle and, beginning Rnd 1,
join CO sts together, making sure that sts do not
become twisted on needle.

Note: Always keep unworked yarn on the WS of
your work.

Rnd 1: P.

Rnd 2: Attach Amethyst and *K1 with Amethyst, K1
with White; rep from * for entire rnd.

Rnd 3: *P1 with Amethyst, K1 with White; rep from
* for entire rnd.

Rnds 4–8: Rep Rnd 3.

Cut Amethyst and with White, K1 rnd. P1 rnd.

Cut White. Attach Light Spring Green and Cream.

Rnd 1: *K1 with Light Spring Green, K1 with
Cream; rep from * for entire rnd.

Rnd 2: *K1 with Light Spring Green, P1 with
Cream; rep from * for entire rnd.

Rnds 3–7: Rep Rnd 2.

Cut Light Spring Green and with Cream, K1 rnd. P1
rnd.

Cut Cream. Attach Light Pink and Amethyst.

With Light Pink, K2 rnds.

*With Amethyst, MB (see p. 114). Drop Amethyst
and with Light Pink, K4; rep from * for entire rnd.

Cut Amethyst. With Light Pink, K until entire piece
measures 5 in.

DRAWSTRING HOLES

*K2tog, YO, K9; rep from * for entire rnd.

K2 rnds.

SEED STITCH RUFFLE

Work Seed st for 2 in. BO all sts.

With Light Spring Green and holding the hat with RS facing and the Seed Stitch Ruffle turned down toward RS, pick up 100 sts around top of hat where Seed st began. K4 rnds.

Dec Rnd 1: *K8, K2tog; rep from * for entire rnd.

Dec Rnd 2: *K7, K2tog; rep from * for entire rnd.

Continue in established pattern, placing sts on dpns when necessary and knitting 1 less st between decs until you have approx 4–6 sts on needles. Cut the yarn, leaving a 6-in. tail. Thread a tapestry needle and pass it through the remaining sts on the needle. Secure the tail on the WS of the work.

With Pale Lemon Yellow, CO 4 sts and create an I-Cord (see p. 115) approx 10 in. long. Thread between drawstring holes, having both drawstring ends meet at the center/front hole.

FLOWERS (MAKE 3)

Note: Make 3 flowers using chenille yarn colors of your choice.

With straight needles and chenille yarn, CO 5 sts.

Row 1 (RS): K.

Rows 2 & all even rows (WS): P.

Row 3: *K1f&b of each st—10 sts.

Row 5: *K1f&b of each st—20 sts.

Row 7: *K1f&b of each st—40 sts.

Row 8: P.

BO all sts.

Stems

With Light Spring Green, CO 3 sts and create three I-Cord flower stems approx 4–6 in. long. Attach to crown of hat.

FINISHING

Twist flowers to create a spiral. Attach each flower to a stem, securing all tails on WS of work.

Father's Day Crown Cap

In honor of this special day, crown your little prince or princess. Glitter yarn serves as the crown jewels that top off each point of this precious hat.

Sizing

Small with 8 points (16-in. circumference)

Large with 6 points (18-in. circumference)

Figures for larger size are given below in parentheses. Where only one set of figures appears, the directions apply to both sizes.

Yarn

DK Weight smooth yarn

The hat shown is made with Tahki Cotton Classic: 100% mercerized cotton, 1.75 oz. (50 g)/108 yd. (100 m).

Yardage

50 (60) yd. #3532 Pale Lemon Yellow

30 (40) yd. #3812 Light Blue or #3446 Light Pink

25 (30) yd. #3722 Light Spring Green

Small amount of glitter yarn

Materials

16-in. U.S. size 4 circular needle

Four U.S. size 4 double-pointed needles

Stitch marker

Tapestry needle

GAUGE

22 sts = 4 in.

Directions

CROWN BASE

With circ needle and Light Spring Green, CO 80 (108) sts.

Place a st marker on right needle and, beginning with Rnd 1, join CO sts together, making sure that sts do not become twisted on needle.

Note: Always keep unworked yarn on the WS of your work and sl sts pw.

Rnd 1: P.

Rnd 2: Attach Light Pink/Light Blue. *K1 with Light Pink/Light Blue, K1 with Light Spring Green; rep from * to end of rnd.

Rnd 3: *K1 with Light Pink/Light Blue, P1 with Light Spring Green; rep from * to end of rnd.

Rnds 4–6: Rep Rnd 3.

Cut Light Pink/Light Blue and with Light Spring Green, K1 rnd. P1 rnd.

Cut Light Spring Green and attach Pale Lemon Yellow.

Knit until entire piece measures 2½ (4) in. from base.

FRONT CROWN POINTS
Small Crown

Row 1: K10. Turn work, leaving the remaining unworked sts on needle.

Row 2 & all even rows: P.

Row 3: *K1, ssk, K to last 3 sts, K2tog, K1. Turn work.

Row 5: K. Turn work.

Row 7: K1, ssk, K to last 3 sts, K2tog, K1. Turn work.

Row 9: K2tog.

BO. Cut yarn.*

Attach yarn at next set of live sts and begin another crown point, starting with Row 1. Cont until you have worked all sts on needle and you have created 8 crown points.

Large Crown

Row 1: K18. Turn work, leaving the rem unworked sts on needle.

Row 2 & all even rows: P18.

Row 3: **K1, SSK, K to last 3 sts, K2tog, K1. Turn work.

Row 4: P.

Continue with established dec pattern on knit rows only until you have 3 sts on needle. BO. Cut yarn.**

Attach yarn at next set of live sts and begin another crown point, starting with Row 1. Continue until you have worked all sts on needle and you have created 6 crown points.

BACK CROWN POINTS

Holding the hat with RS facing you, bend the Pale Lemon Yellow crown point down and expose the crown base. With Pale Lemon Yellow, pick up 10 (18) sts evenly across the base of one crown point.

K1 row. P1 row.

Rep from * (**) to * (**) of Front Crown Points to create the back of the point, making sure that WS are facing each other and RS are facing out.

Rep for the rem 7 (5) points.

Using the tails of the points and a tapestry needle, sew all points together. Weave in all loose ends.

CROWN PEAK

Hold the hat with RS facing you, bending all crown points away from you. With Light Pink/Light Blue, pick up 80 (108) sts evenly around the hat. Place st marker at beginning of round and K10 (12) rnds.

DECREASE ROUNDS

Next dec rnd: *K8, K2tog; rep from * to end of rnd.

Next dec rnd: *K7, K2tog; rep from * to end of rnd.

Continue in established dec pattern, knitting 1 less st between dec and switching to dpns when necessary until 5 sts rem.

Cut the yarn, leaving a 6-in. tail. Using a tapestry needle, thread the tail through the rem sts on the needle, then secure the tail on the WS of the work.

FINISHING

With Light Spring Green, sew a small, even running st along the base of the crown to help the points stand up tall.

Crown Jewels

With glitter yarn, CO 5 sts.

Work 5 rows in Garter st to create a square. Cut yarn, leaving a 6-in. tail. Using a tapestry needle, thread the tail through the rem sts on the needle, then carefully slip needle along the edge of each side of the square. Pull tightly, creating a small round bobble. Use the tail to attach to the tip of each point on the crown.

Summer and Other Celebrations

Firecracker Topper

What a great hat for the summertime! A traditional sailor shape with a sizzling, glittery topper will bring a little pizzazz to any Fourth of July celebration.

Sizing

Small (14-in. circumference)

Large (18-in. circumference)

Figures for larger size are given below in parentheses. Where only one set of figures appears, the directions apply to both sizes.

Yarn

DK Weight smooth yarn

DK Weight eyelash yarn

The hat shown is made with S.R. Kertzer Super 10 Cotton: 100% mercerized cotton, 4.4 oz. (125 g)/250 yd. (228.6 m) and Stylecraft Icicle: 62% polyester, 38% metallized polyester, 1.75 oz. (50 g)/87 yd. (80 m).

Yardage

40 (50) yd. Super 10 Cotton #3997 Scarlet

30 (40) yd. Super 10 Cotton White

30 (40) yd. Super 10 Cotton #3871 Royal

20 yd. Super 10 Cotton #3533 Daffodil

2 yd. Icicle #1141 Polar

Materials

16-in. U.S. size 4 circular needle

Four U.S. size 4 double-pointed needles

Two stitch markers

Tapestry needle

GAUGE

22 sts = 4 in. with Super 10 Cotton

SEED STITCH

Rnd 1: *K1, P1; rep from * to end of rnd.

All other rnds: K the P sts and P the K sts.

Directions

HAT BASE

Using circ needles and Scarlet, CO 82 (100) sts. Place a st marker on right needle and, beginning Rnd 1, join CO sts together, making sure that sts do not become twisted on needle.

Note: Always keep unworked yarn on the WS of your work and sl sts pw.

Rnd 1: P.

Rnd 2: Drop Scarlet and attach White. With White, *K1, sl 1 wyib; rep from * to end of rnd.

Rnd 3: With White, *P1, sl 1 wyib; rep from * to end of rnd.

Rnd 4: Drop White. K with Scarlet for entire rnd.

Rnd 5: P with Scarlet.

Rep Rnds 2–5 twice.

Cut White, and with Scarlet work Seed st for 1½ (2½) in. Cut Scarlet and attach Daffodil. K1 rnd. Bind off pw.

Holding the hat with the RS facing you, bend the Seed st work down to expose the WS of the hat base. You will see the White and Scarlet loops from the initial ribbing. With Royal, pick up 82 (100) sts (the loops) evenly spaced around the hat. *K4 rnds. Drop Royal and attach White. K4 rnds. Rep from * until you have 3 Royal stripes. Cut Royal and attach Scarlet. K1 rnd, P1 rnd, placing a second st marker halfway across work.

DECREASE ROUNDS

**Drop Scarlet and pick up White.

Dec Rnd: *K to 2 sts before marker, K2tog, sl marker, sl 1, K1, psso. Rep from * at second marker.

Rep Dec Rnd twice more, for a total of 3 Dec Rnds.

RIDGE ROUND

Drop White and pick up Scarlet. K1 rnd, P1 rnd. Rep from **, dec at the markers on every White rnd and placing sts on dpns when necessary. Work until you have created 6 Scarlet ridges and you have approx 8 sts left on the needles. Cut the yarn, leaving a 6-in. tail. Using a tapestry needle, thread the tail through the remaining sts on the needles. Pull the yarn, gathering sts tightly together, then secure the tail on the WS of the hat.

FIRECRACKER TOPPER

Cut 10–15 Icicle strands (approx 6 in. long) and tie them together at the center using a strand of Icicle. Fold this bundle in half, making a tassel, and secure it to the tip of the hat by tying the tails to the WS of the hat.

FINISHING

Weave in all ends. Make five 2-in.-long I-Cords (see p. 115) with Daffodil. Using a tapestry needle, thread the I-Cord tail through to the same end as the CO tail. Use both tails to attach each I-Cord to the tip of the hat.

Fold the Scarlet Seed st "ruffle" down to the bottom of the hat to create a faux welt for the base of the hat.

Fourth of July Top Hat

No patriotic hat would be complete without the fireworks. This top hat also has a knit lining that will help make your stars and stripes stand tall and proud.

Sizing

Small (18-in. circumference)

Large (20-in. circumference)

Figures for larger size are given below in parentheses. Where only one set of figures appears, the directions apply to both sizes.

Yarn

DK Weight smooth yarn

The hat shown is made with Tahki Cotton Classic: 100% mercerized cotton, 1.75 oz. (50 g)/108 yd. (100 m).

Yardage

120 (160) yd. #3424 Deep Red

80 (120) yd. #3001 White

60 (80) yd. #3873 Dark Royal Blue

60 yd. #3533 Bright Yellow

Materials

16-in. U.S. size 4 circular needle

Five U.S. size 4 double-pointed needles

Stitch marker

Tapestry needle

GAUGE

22 sts = 4 in.

Directions

HAT BASE

With circ needle and Deep Red, CO 90 (110) sts. Place a st marker on right needle and, beginning Rnd 1, join CO sts together, making sure that sts do not become twisted on needle.

Row 1: P.

K10 rows.

Drop Deep Red and attach Dark Royal Blue.

Rnd 1: K.

Rnd 2: P.

Rnds 3–9: K.

Rnd 10: P.

Cut Dark Royal Blue and pick up Deep Red.

K8 rnds.

Drop Deep Red and attach White.

K8 rnds.

Rep the Deep Red and White stripes until you have a total of 2 White bands and 3 Deep Red bands.

RIDGE ROUND

Cut White. Drop Deep Red and attach Bright Yellow.

K1 rnd. P1 rnd. Cut Bright Yellow and pick up Deep Red.

LINING

With Deep Red, knit until lining is the same length as the Hat Base. BO all sts.

CROWN OF HAT

Fold the Deep Red lining inside at the Bright Yellow Ridge Rnd. With Dark Royal Blue, pick up 90 (110) sts evenly around top edge of hat.

With Dark Royal Blue, K10 rnds.

Cut Dark Royal Blue and attach White.

DECREASE CROWN

Dec Rnd 1: With White, *K8, K2tog; rep from * for entire rnd.

Dec Rnd 2: *K7, K2tog; rep from * for entire rnd.

Continue in established pattern, knitting 1 less st between dec and placing sts on dpns when necessary for a total of 6 rnds.

Cut White and attach Deep Red. Continue decreasing until you have approx 4–6 sts on needles. Cut the yarn, leaving a 6-in. tail. Using a tapestry needle, thread the tail through the rem sts on the needle. Pull the yarn, gathering sts tightly together, then secure the tail on the WS of the work.

WELT

Thread a tapestry needle with Bright Yellow, pinch the hat at the Bright Yellow top Ridge Rnd, and create a Welt (see p. 116) by sewing together the top and bottom pieces using even running stitches.

STARS (MAKE 6)

With Bright Yellow and straight needles, CO 50 sts.

Row 1: *K4, sl2tog kw, K1, p2sso, K3; rep from * to end of row—40 sts.

Row 2: K3, *sl1wyif, K7; rep from * to last 3 sts, K3.

Row 3: K3, *sl2tog kw, K1, p2sso, k5; rep from * to last 2 sts, K2—30 sts.

Row 4: K2, *sl1wyif, K5; rep from * to last 3 sts, K3.

Row 5: K2, *sl2tog kw, K1, p2sso, K4; rep from * to last st, K1—20 sts.

Row 6: K1, *sl1wyif, K3; rep from * to last 2 sts, K2.

Row 7: K1, *sl2tog kw, k1, p2sso, K1; rep from * to last 2 sts, sl2tog kw, p2sso—10 sts.

Row 8: *Sl1wyif, K1; rep from * to end of row.

Row 9: K2tog across entire row. BO all 5 sts.

FIREWORKS (MAKE 6)

CO 18 sts.

Row 1: K1 into the front, back, and front again of each st, creating 3 sts in each st.

BO all sts pw.

FINISHING

Weave in all loose ends. With Bright Yellow, create French Knots (see p. 115) along Dark Royal Blue base.

Sew Deep Red lining to inside of hat. Fold bottom Dark Royal Blue ridge row and sew Deep Red lining at bottom to inside.

Wind each Firework into a tight spiral. Attach Fireworks securely to top of hat. Sew Stars together, WS facing, and attach to three of the Fireworks for the patriotic show to begin!

Birthday Cupcake Cap

This sugar-coated hat is so sweet you'll want to eat it up! With French Knots, you create festive sprinkles, and the candle in the middle has a little glittery flame to help celebrate the special day.

Sizing

One size (14-in. circumference)

Yarn

DK Weight smooth yarn

DK Weight eyelash yarn

Bulky Weight bouclé yarn

The hat shown is made with S.R. Kertzer Super 10 Cotton: 100% mercerized cotton, 4.4 oz. (125 g)/250 yd. (228.6 m); Stylecraft Icicle: 62% polyester, 38% metallized polyester, 1.75 oz. (50 g)/87 yd. (80 m); and Lion Brand Homespun®: 98% acrylic, 2% polyester, 6 oz. (170 g)/185 yd./(169 m).

Yardage

60 yd. Super 10 Cotton #3446 Cotton Candy or #3841 Caribbean

3 yd. Super 10 Cotton #3997 Scarlet

5 yd. Super 10 Cotton White

2 yd. Homespun #790-389 Spring Green

30 yd. Icicle #1143 Sunlight

Materials

16-in. U.S. size 4 circular needle

Four U.S. size 4 double-pointed needles

Stitch marker

Tapestry needle

GAUGE

22 sts = 4 in. with Super 10 Cotton

SEED STITCH

Rnd 1: *K1, P1; rep from * to end of rnd.

All other rnds: K the P sts and P the K sts.

Directions

HAT BASE

With circ needles and Cotton Candy/Caribbean, CO 72 sts. Place a st marker on right needle and, beginning Rnd 1, join CO sts together, making sure that sts do not become twisted on needle.

Rnd 1: P.

Work Seed st for 3 in.

Cut Cotton Candy/Caribbean and attach
   Homespun.
K1 rnd. P1 rnd.
Cut Homespun and attach Icicle.

CROWN

With Icicle, work Seed st on all rnds for approx 2 in.

DECREASE ROUNDS

Dec Rnd 1: *K7, K2tog; rep from * to end of rnd.
Dec Rnd 2: *K6, K2tog; rep from * to end of rnd.
Dec Rnd 3: *K5, K2tog; rep from * to end of rnd.
Continue in established pattern, knitting one less
   st between dec and changing to dpns when
   necessary. Cut yarn, leaving a 6-in. tail. Using
   a tapestry needle, thread the tail through the rem
   sts on the needles. Pull the yarn, gathering sts
   tightly together, then secure the tail on the WS
   of work.

BIRTHDAY CANDLE

With 2 dpns and White, CO 7 sts.
Work I-Cord (see p. 115) for 14 rnds.
Cut White, attach Icicle, and work 3 rnds.
Cut Icicle and, using a tapestry needle, thread the
   Icicle and White tails through the rem sts on
   the needle and pass all tails through the inside
   of the I-Cord.
Using those tails, attach the candle securely to the
   tip of the hat for a candle that will never burn out!

Make French Knots (see p. 115) with Scarlet to
   create sprinkles on the top of your cupcake.

WELT

Thread a tapestry needle with White, pinch the hat
   at the Homespun pure rnd, and create a Welt
   (see p. 116) by sewing together the top and
   bottom pieces using even running stitches.

FINISHING

Weave in all loose ends. Now it's birthday time!

A Slice of Birthday Cake Cap

Little ones can party in style with this sweet confection of a hat. What better way to celebrate a birthday than with a glittery candle atop a slice of cake?

Sizing

Small (16-in. circumference)

Large (18-in. circumference)

Figures for larger size are given below in parentheses. Where only one set of figures appears, the directions apply to both sizes.

Yarn

DK Weight smooth yarn

The hat shown is made with Tahki Cotton Classic: 100% mercerized cotton, 1.75 oz. (50 g)/ 108 yd. (100 m).

Yardage

40 (50) yd. Cotton Classic #3548 Butter Yellow

50 (70) yd. Cotton Classic #3446 Light Pink or #3812 Light Blue

30 yd. Cotton Classic #3722 Light Spring Green

10 yd. Cotton Classic #3248 Milk Chocolate

20 yd. Cotton Classic #3001 White

35 yd. yellow satin rattail cord

Small amount of glitter yarn for candle

Materials

16-in. U.S. size 4 circular needle

Five U.S. size 4 double-pointed needles

Stitch marker

Tapestry needle

Small amount of polyester filling

GAUGE

22 sts = 4 in.

Directions

HAT BASE

With circ needle and Butter Yellow, CO 90 (110) sts. Place a st marker on right needle and, beginning Rnd 1, join CO sts together making sure that sts do not become twisted on needle.

Note: Always keep unworked yarn on the WS of your work and sl sts pw.

Rnd 1: P.

Rnd 2: Drop Butter Yellow and with Light Spring Green, *K1, sl 1 wyib; rep from * to end of rnd.

Rnd 3: *P1, sl 1 wyib; rep from * to end of rnd.

Rnd 4: Drop Light Spring Green and K entire rnd with Butter Yellow.

Rnd 5: P.

Rep Rnds 2–5 two more times, ending with a completed Rnd 5.

Cut Light Spring Green and Butter Yellow and attach Light Pink/Light Blue.

K until entire piece measures 3 (4) in.

FIRST RIDGE ROUND

Drop Light Pink/Light Blue and attach yellow silk rattail cord.

K1 rnd. P1 rnd.

Drop yellow silk rattail cord and attach Light Pink/Light Blue.

K10 (15) rnds.

DECREASE ROUNDS

Next Dec Rnd: *K8, K2tog; rep from * to end of rnd.

K4 (5) rnds.

Next Dec Rnd: *K7, K2tog; rep from * to end of rnd.

K4 (5) rnds.

Continue in established pattern, knitting 1 less st between dec and changing to dpns when necessary until you have completed the dec of K5, K2tog.

SECOND RIDGE ROUND

Cut Light Pink/Light Blue and attach yellow silk rattail cord.

K1 rnd. P1 rnd.

Drop yellow silk rattail cord and attach Light Spring Green.

K1 rnd. P1 rnd.

Cut Light Spring Green and pick up yellow silk rattail cord.

K1 rnd. P1 rnd.

Cut yellow silk rattail cord. Attach Butter Yellow.

K10 (15) rnds.

HAT CROWN DECREASE ROUNDS

Dec Rnd 1: *K4, K2tog; rep from * to end of rnd.

Dec Rnd 2: *K3, K2tog; rep from * to end of rnd.

Continue in established pattern, knitting 1 less st between dec until you have approx 3–5 sts on needles. Cut the yarn, leaving a 6-in. tail. Using a tapestry needle, thread the tail through the rem sts on the needle. Pull the yarn, gathering sts tightly together, then secure the tail on the WS of work.

CHOCOLATE CAKE SLICE

Top of Cake Slice

With straight needles and Milk Chocolate, CO 30 sts.

Row 1: P.

Row 2: *K4, K2tog; rep from * to end of row.

Row 3: *P2tog, P3; rep from * to end of row.

Row 4: *K2, K2tog; rep from * to end of row.

Row 5: P.

Row 6: P.

Starting with a K row, continue in St st for 10 rows. P2 rows.

Bottom of Cake Slice

Rows 1, 3, 7 & 9 (RS): *K1, ssk, K to last 3 sts, K2tog, K1.

Rows 2, 4, 6 & 8 (WS): P.

Row 5: K.

Continue with established dec pattern until 3 sts remain. K3tog and fasten off.

Cake Slice Frosting

With WS facing and point of wedge facing down, use Milk Chocolate to pick up 15 sts along P ridge where the frosting edge meets the back.

K1 row. Work same as Rows 1–9 of Bottom of Cake Slice.

Cake Slice Sides

With RS facing and using White, pick up 14 sts along one cake slice top.

Work in St st for 4 rows. Drop White and attach Light Pink/Light Blue for center frosting.

K1 row. P1 row. Cut Light Pink/Light Blue. Pick up White and work another 4 rows. BO all sts.

Rep for other side of cake. Carefully sew sides, making sure the point meets with the middle frosting. Stuff with polyester filling.

CANDLE

With Light Pink/Light Blue, create a 4-st I-Cord (see p. 115) for desired length of candle. Attach to top of cake.

FINISHING

With a small amount of glitter yarn, create a "flame" with a small French Knot (see p. 115) on top of candle.

Attach Cake Slice to top of hat.

With Light Spring Green, create French Knots all over the base of the hat. Weave in all loose ends.

Now that you've lit the candle, you are ready to celebrate!

Glitter & Glow Beanie

This sweet and elegant beanie is a snap to make. Tie it up with a giant fancy ribbon and make a delightful present out of the precious newborn you have in mind!

Sizing

One size (16-in. circumference)

Yarn

DK Weight smooth yarn

DK Weight eyelash yarn

The hat shown is made with S.R. Kertzer Super 10 Cotton: 100% mercerized cotton, 4.4 oz. (125 g)/250 yd. (228.6 m) and Stylecraft Icicle: 62% polyester, 38% metallized polyester, 1.75 oz. (50 g)/87 yd. (80 m).

Yardage

50 yd. Super 10 Cotton #3446 Cotton Candy or #3841 Caribbean

30 yd. Super 10 Cotton #3532 Soft Yellow

40 yd. Icicle #1140 Crystal or #1142 Sunlight

Materials

16-in. U.S. size 4 circular needle

1-in.-wide ribbon, 10 in. long

Stitch marker

Tapestry needle

GAUGE

22 sts = 4 in. with Super 10 Cotton

SEED STITCH

Rnd 1: *K1, P1; rep from * to end of rnd.

All other rnds: K the P sts and P the K sts.

Directions

HAT BASE

With circ needles and Cotton Candy/Caribbean, CO 72 sts. Place a st marker on right needle and, beginning Rnd 1, join CO sts together, making sure that sts do not become twisted on needle.

Rnd 1: P.

Work Seed st for 4 in.

Drop Cotton Candy/Caribbean and attach Soft Yellow. *K1 rnd, P1 rnd. Rep from * once.

STRIPED TOP

Rnd 1: *K2 with Cotton Candy/Caribbean. Drop Cotton Candy/Caribbean and, keeping yarn in the back of your work, K2 with Soft Yellow; rep from * for entire rnd.

Rnd 2: *K2 with Cotton Candy/Caribbean. P2 with Soft Yellow; rep from * for entire rnd.

Rep Rnd 2 for 15 rnds.

Next Rnd: Cut Soft Yellow and with Cotton Candy/Caribbean, K entire rnd.

Eyelet Rnd: *K1, YO, K2tog, K5; rep from * to end of rnd.

Next Rnd: K entire rnd.

Cut Cotton Candy/Caribbean and attach Crystal/Sunlight.

K1 rnd. P1 rnd.

SQUIGGLES

Step 1: Using the Cable Cast-On (see p. 114), CO 6 sts.

Step 2: BO those 6 sts.

Step 3: K6 sts from hat top.

Rep these 3 steps for entire rnd. BO all sts.

FINISHING

Weave in all loose ends. Thread a sweet ribbon through the eyelets and tie a big, beautiful bow on top of the hat. It'll be an instant sensation!

Crystal Party Hat

This shimmery, iridescent hat is sure to shine all day and night.
Knit it up in daffodil yellow or girly girl pink.

Sizing

One size (15-in. circumference)

Yarn

DK Weight smooth yarn

DK Weight eyelash yarn

DK Weight tufted yarn

The hat shown is made with S.R. Kertzer Super 10
Cotton: 100% mercerized cotton, 4.4 oz.
(125 g)/250 yd. (228.6 m); Stylecraft Icicle:
62% polyester, 38% metallized polyester, 1.75 oz.
(50 g)/87 yd. (80 m); and Stylecraft Marrakech:
79% nylon, 21% acrylic, 1.75 oz. (50 g)/
109 yd. (100 m).

Yardage

50 yd. Super 10 Cotton #3533 Daffodil or #3446
Cotton Candy

50 yd. Icicle #1142 Sunlight

30 yd. Marrakech #1158 Seaspray

Materials

16-in. U.S. size 4 circular needle

Four U.S. size 4 double-pointed needles

Stitch marker

Tapestry needle

GAUGE

22 sts = 4 in. with Super 10 Cotton

Directions

HAT BASE

With circ needles and Sunlight, CO 72 sts. Place
a st marker on right needle and, beginning Rnd
1, join CO sts together, making sure sts do not
become twisted on needle.

Rnd 1: P.

Rnd 2: K.

Rep Rnds 1 and 2 until work measures
approx 1½ in.

FIRST RIDGE ROUND

Drop Sunlight and attach Seaspray.

Rnd 1: K.

Rnd 2: P.

Drop Seaspray and pick up Sunlight.

Rnd 3: K.

Rnd 4: P.

Drop Sunlight and attach Daffodil/Cotton Candy.

Rnd 5: K.

FIRST DECREASE ROUND

Dec Rnd 1: *With Daffodil/Cotton Candy *K7, K2tog; rep from * to end of rnd.

K3 rnds.

SECOND RIDGE ROUND

**Drop Daffodil/Cotton Candy and pick up Sunlight.

Rnd 1: K.

Rnd 2: P.

Drop Icicle and pick up Seaspray.

Rnd 3: K.

Rnd 4: P.

Drop Seaspray and pick up Sunlight.

Rnd 5: K.

Rnd 6: P.

Drop Sunlight and pick up Daffodil/Cotton Candy.

Rnd 7: K.

SECOND DECREASE ROUND

Dec Rnd 1: *With Daffodil/Cotton Candy *K6, K2tog; rep from * to end of rnd.

K3 rnds.

Rep from ** for remainder of hat.

Continue in established pattern, knitting 1 less st

between decs until you have completed the dec rnd of K2, K2tog. You should have a total of 7 Ridge Rounds.

With Daffodil/Cotton Candy, K2tog for an entire rnd until 6 sts rem. Cut Daffodil/Cotton Candy and Icicle. With Seaspray, make an I-Cord (see p. 115) approx 6 in. long.

Cut Seaspray, attach Sunlight, and continue I-Cord for 1 in. Cut yarn leaving a 6-in. tail. Use a tapestry needle to draw tail through the remaining sts, then down into the center of the cord.

FINISHING

Weave in all loose ends. Make a knot with the I-Cord and make sure the Sunlight tip peeks out to glow and glisten on top!

Fabulous Fall

Arbor Day Cap

Help celebrate Arbor Day with this adorable hat that features a base of scalloped leaves, swirls of grass, and a cherry tree topper. It's a great hat for a little tree hugger!

Sizing

Small (14-in. circumference)

Large (16-in. circumference)

Figures for larger size are given below in parentheses. Where only one set of figures appears, the directions apply to both sizes.

Yarn

DK Weight smooth yarn

The yarn shown is made with Lion Brand LB Collection Superwash Merino: 100% superwash merino, 3.5 oz. (100 g)/306 yd. (280 m).

Yardage

30 (40) yd. Superwash Merino #486-114 Cayenne

50 (60) yd. Superwash Merino #486-170 Dijon

20 (35) yd. Superwash Merino #486-174 Spring Leaf

40 (50) yd. Superwash Merino #486-127 Mahogany

30 (40) yd. Superwash Merino #486-141 Wild Berry

Materials

16-in. U.S. size 4 circular needle

Four U.S. size 4 double-pointed needles

One pair U.S. size 4 straight needles

Stitch marker

Tapestry needle

GAUGE

22 sts = 4 in.

SEED STITCH

Rnd 1: *K1, P1; rep from * to end of rnd.

All other rnds: K the P sts and P the K sts.

Directions

HAT BASE LEAF EDGING

With Dijon and straight needles, CO 8 sts.

Row 1 (RS): K5, YO, K1, YO, K2—10 sts.

Row 2 (WS): P6, K1f&b, K3—11 sts.

Row 3: K4, P1, K2, YO, K1, YO, K3—13 sts.

Row 4: P8, K1f&b, K4—14 sts.

Row 5: K4, P2, K3, YO, K1, YO, K4—16 sts.

Row 6: P10, K1f&b, K5—17 sts.

Row 7: K4, P3, K4, YO, K1, YO, K5—19 sts.

Row 8: P12, K1f&b, K6—20 sts.

Row 9: K4, P4, ssk, K7, K2tog, K1—18 sts.

Row 10: P10, K1f&b, K7—19 sts.

Row 11: K4, P5, ssk, K5, K2tog, K1—17 sts.

Row 12: P8, K1f&b, K2, P1, K5—18 sts.

Row 13: K4, P1, K1, P4, ssk, K3, K2tog, K1—16 sts.

Row 14: P6, K1f&b, K3, P1, K5—17 sts.

Row 15: K4, P1, K1, P5, ssk, K1, K2tog, K1—15 sts.

Row 16: P4, K1f&b, K4, P1, K5—16 sts.

Row 17: K4, P1, K1, P6, sl 1, K2tog, psso, K1—14 sts.

Row 18: P2tog, BO 5 sts, P3, K4—8 sts.

Rep Rows 1–18 nine (ten) times.

BO all sts.

With tapestry needle, carefully sew pieces together to create the base.

HAT BODY

Holding the Leaf Edging piece with RS facing, bend the leaf edge toward you to expose the ridge of sts between the leaves and the Garter st ridge base of the edging. With circ needle and Mahogany, pick up 80 (100) sts evenly around the hat. Place a st marker on right needle and K1 row. Work in Seed st until the piece measures 1½ (1¾) in.

SPRING LEAF RIDGE ROWS

Drop Mahogany and attach Spring Leaf.

With Spring Leaf, K1 rnd, P1 rnd.

*Drop Spring Leaf and pick up Mahogany. K1 rnd. Continue with Seed st for 5 (7) rnds.

Drop Mahogany and pick up Spring Leaf.

Decrease rnd: **K8, K2tog; rep from * for entire rnd.

With Spring Leaf, P1 rnd.**

Rep from ** to **, knitting 1 less st between dec until you have completed a total of 4 Spring Leaf ridges.

CROWN

Cut Mahogany and Spring Leaf, leaving a 6-in. tail for both. Attach Cayenne and K1 rnd.

Work Seed st for ½ (1) in.

K2tog until 4–6 sts remain, changing to dpns when necessary. Cut the yarn, leaving a 6-in. tail. Using a tapestry needle, thread the tail through the remaining sts left on the needle. Pull the yarn, gathering sts tightly together, then secure the tail on the WS of the work.

TREE TOPPER (MAKE 2)

Note: The tree is worked from the top down.

Top of Tree

With Spring Leaf, CO 1 st.

Row 1: (K1, P1, K1) in same st—3 sts.

Row 2: K1, P1, K1.

Row 3: K1f&b, P1, K1f&b—5 sts.

Row 4: (P1, K1) twice, P1.

Row 5: K1f&b, K1, P1, K1, K1f&b—7 sts.

Row 6: K1 (P1, K1) 3 times.

Rows 7–14: Continue inc 1 st (K1f&b) at beg and end of every other row. You will have 15 sts after completing Row 14.

K1 row.

BO 5 sts, K4, BO 5 sts. Cut yarn.

Trunk of Tree

Attach Dijon and, working with rem 5 sts, work in K1, P1 rib for 1½ in. BO all sts.

With Cayenne, create small French Knots (see p. 115) on both Seed st tops.

Using the tails of the yarn, stuff the tree and sew both sides together with RS facing. Attach to top of crown.

FINISHING

Weave in all loose ends. Thread a tapestry needle with Cayenne and attach Hat Base Leaf Edging to Hat Body base with French Knots at the tip of each leaf.

Leaf Peeper Cap

Celebrate the colors of the fall by knitting giant leaves and attaching them to a bright yellow cap with orange swirls.

Sizing

Small (14-in. circumference)

Large (18- to 20-in. circumference)

Figures for larger size are given below in
parentheses. Where only one set of figures
appears, the directions apply to both sizes.

Yarn

DK Weight smooth yarn

The hat shown is made with HiKoo Simplicity:
55% superwash merino, 28% acrylic, 17% nylon,
1.75 oz. (50 g)/117 yd. (107 m).

Yardage

90 (100) yd. Simplicity #004 Goldfish

30 yd. Simplicity #034 Orange

30 yd. Simplicity #040 Green Apple

40 (50) yd. Simplicity #016 Gypsy Red

Materials

16-in. U.S. size 4 circular needle

Four U.S. size 4 double-pointed needles

One pair U.S. size 4 straight needles

Stitch marker

Tapestry needle

GAUGE

20 sts = 4 in.

Directions

HAT BASE

Using circ needle and Goldfish, CO 80 (100) sts.

Place a st marker on right needle and, beginning
Rnd 1, join CO sts together, making sure that sts
do not become twisted on needle.

Rnd 1: P.

First Tier

Rnd 1: Attach Gypsy Red. *K1 with Goldfish, K1
with Gypsy Red; rep from * to end of rnd.

Rnd 2: Drop Goldfish. *Sl1 wyib, P1 with Gypsy

Red; rep from * to end of rnd.

Rnd 3: *K1 with Goldfish, P1 with Gypsy Red; rep from * to end of rnd.

Rnds 4 & 5: Rep Rnd 3.

Rnd 6: K with Goldfish.

Rnd 7: P with Goldfish.

Rep First Tier Rnds 1–7.

Cut Gypsy Red and pick up Goldfish. Continue in Stockinette st until entire piece measures 3 (4) in.

RIDGE ROWS

Drop Goldfish and attach Gypsy Red.

K1 rnd. P1 rnd.

Cut Gypsy Red and pick up Goldfish.

K1 rnd. P1 rnd.

Attach Orange and drop Goldfish.

K1 rnd. P1 rnd.

Decrease Rows

Note: Place sts on dpns when necessary.

Dec Rnd 1: *K8, K2tog; rep from * to end of rnd.

Dec Rnd 2: *K7, K2tog; rep from * to end of rnd.

Dec Rnd 3: *K6, K2tog; rep from * to end of rnd.

Dec Rnd 4: *K5, K2tog; rep from * to end of rnd.

Dec Rnd 5 and all other rnds: K2tog. When you have approx 4–8 sts remaining, work I-Cord (see p. 115) for 2 in. Cut, leaving a 6-in. tail. Thread a tapestry needle and pass it through the rem sts on the needle. Secure the tail on the WS of the work.

LEAVES

Create 4 leaves each in Gypsy Red, Orange, and Green Apple for a total of 12 leaves as follows:

With straight needles and desired color, CO 5 sts. K1 row, P1 row.

Row 1 (RS): *K1f&b, YO, K1, YO, K1, YO, K2—9 sts.

Rows 2, 4, 6, 10, 12 & 16 (WS): P.

Rows 3 & 9: K4, YO, K1, YO, K4—11 sts.

Rows 5 & 11: K5, YO, K1, YO, K5—13 sts.

Row 7: BO 3 sts, K2, YO, K1, YO, K6—12 sts.

Row 8: BO 3 sts, P8—9 sts.

Row 13: BO 3 sts, K9—10 sts.

Row 14: BO 3 sts, P6—7 sts.

Row 15: Sl1, K1, psso, K3, K2tog—5 sts.

Row 17: Sl1, K1, psso, K1, K2tog—3 sts.

Row 18: BO all sts.

Sew 2 leaves of the same color together with WS facing to make 1 large leaf.

FINISHING

Attach one of each color leaf at top of hat, alternating the colors. Attach a second layer of leaves, one of each color, on top of the first layer of leaves, sewing them to the I-Cord to create the effect of the leaves standing up on their own.

Using Duplicate Stitch (see p. 114) and Orange, create diagonal swirls.

Halloween Hat

Whose little pumpkin wouldn't love this little pumpkin hat? The eyes and mouth are made with a Duplicate Stitch, so create any expression you want on this trick-or-treat topper.

Sizing

Small (14-in. circumference)

Large (16-in. circumference)

Figures for larger size are given below in parentheses. Where only one set of figures appears, the directions apply to both sizes.

Yarn

DK Weight smooth yarn

The hat shown is made with S.R. Kertzer Super 10 Cotton: 100% mercerized cotton, 4.4 oz. (125 g)/250 yd. (228.6 m).

Yardage

70 (80) yd. Super 10 Cotton #3402 Nectarine

30 (40) yd. Super 10 Cotton #3764 Peppermint

10 yd. Super 10 Cotton #3553 Canary

2 yd. Super 10 Cotton #3327 Chocolate

Materials

16-in. U.S. size 3 circular needle

Four U.S. size 3 double-pointed needles

11 stitch markers

Tapestry needle

GAUGE

22 sts = 4 in.

Directions

HAT BASE

With circ needle and Peppermint, CO 74 (88) sts. Place a st marker on right needle and, beginning Rnd 1, join CO sts together, making sure that sts do not become twisted on needle.

Note: Always keep the unworked yarn on the WS of the work and sl sts pw.

Rnd 1: P.

Rnd 2: Drop Peppermint and attach Nectarine. With Nectarine, *K1, sl 1 wyib; rep from * to end of rnd.

Rnd 3: With Nectarine, *P1, sl 1 wyib; rep from * to end of rnd.

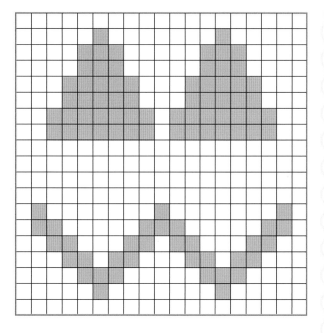

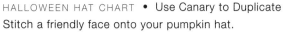

HALLOWEEN HAT CHART • Use Canary to Duplicate Stitch a friendly face onto your pumpkin hat.

Rnd 4: Drop Nectarine. K entire rnd with Peppermint.

Rnd 5: P with Peppermint.

Rep Rnds 2–5 twice.

INCREASE ROUND

Cut Peppermint and pick up Nectarine.

Inc Rnd 1: Smaller size: *K1, K1f&b; rep from * to last 2 sts; K2. Larger size: *K1, K1f&b; rep from * for entire rnd. There should be 110 (132) sts on the needle.

RIBBING PATTERN

With Nectarine, *K9 (11), P1; rep from * for entire rnd. Continue with this ribbing pattern for 20 (25) rnds.

RIDGE ROUND

Drop Nectarine and attach Peppermint. K1 rnd. P1 rnd. Drop Peppermint, and with Nectarine work Ribbing Pattern for 6 (8) rnds. Drop Nectarine and attach Peppermint. K1 rnd. P1 rnd.

SWIRL TOP

Drop Peppermint and attach Nectarine. K entire rnd, placing a st marker every 10 (12) sts (after P st of ribbing). For 6 rnds, make the following dec at each marker: Sl marker, sl 1 st, K1 st, psso. Drop Nectarine and attach Peppermint. K1 rnd. P1 rnd.

Cut Peppermint and attach Nectarine. K2tog for the entire rnd until about 4–5 sts rem. Cut Nectarine and attach Chocolate. Work an I-Cord (see p. 115) for approx 10 rnds or until you have the desired length of stem for your pumpkin. Cut the yarn, leaving a 6-in. tail. Using a tapestry needle, thread the tail through the remaining sts on the needle. Bring yarn through the I-Cord to the WS of the work.

FINISHING

Weave in all ends. Using Duplicate Stitch (see p. 114) and Canary, embroider a friendly or ghoulish face onto your pumpkin as shown on the facing page and using the chart above or your own design. Using Nectarine, make French Knots (see p. 115) for bright eyes.

Witch's Hat

Knit baby a hat that looks and feels like a real witch's hat, thanks to a stiff brim at the base and a long, wiggly tail on top.

Sizing

Small (16-in. circumference)

Large (18-in. circumference)

Figures for the larger size are given below in parentheses. Where only one set of figures appears, the directions apply to both sizes.

Yarn

DK Weight smooth yarn

The hat shown is made with Tahki Cotton Classic: 100% mercerized cotton, 1.75 oz. (50 g)/108 yd. (100 m).

Yardage

120 (160) yd. Cotton Classic #3002 Black

40 (50) yd. Cotton Classic #3541 Light Cantaloupe

30 yd. Cotton Classic #3533 Bright Yellow

10 yd. Cotton Classic #3997 Bright Red

Materials

16-in. U.S. size 4 circular needle

Four U.S. size 4 double-pointed needles

Stitch marker

Tapestry needle

Piece of thin cardboard for the brim

Small amount of polyester filling (optional)

GAUGE

22 sts = 4 in.

SEED STITCH

Rnd 1: *K1, P1; rep from * to end of rnd.

All other rnds: K the P sts and P the K sts.

Directions

BRIM

With circ needle and Black, CO 160 (200) sts.

Place a st marker on right needle and, beginning Rnd 1, join CO sts together, making sure that sts do not become twisted on needle.

Rnd 1: P.

Work Seed st until piece measures 2 (2½) in.

RIDGE ROUNDS

K1 rnd. P1 rnd.

Continue with Seed st for another 2 (2½) in.

Next rnd: K2tog entire rnd—80 (100) sts.

K2 rnds.

STRIPED BODY

Note: Place sts on dpns when necessary.

Drop Black and attach Light Cantaloupe. K8 rnds.

Dec Rnd: With Black, *K8, K2tog; rep from * to
   end of rnd.

K7 rnds.

With Light Cantaloupe, *K7, K2tog; rep from * to
   end of rnd.

K7 rnds.

With Black, *K6, K2tog; rep from * to end of rnd.

K7 rnds.

With Light Cantaloupe, *K5, K2tog; rep from * to
   end of rnd.

K7 rnds.

With Black, *K4, K2tog; rep from * to end of rnd.

K3 rnds.

With Light Cantaloupe, K4 rnds.

With Black, *K3, K2tog; rep from * to end of rnd.

K3 rnds.

With Light Cantaloupe, *K2, K2tog; rep from * to
   end of rnd.

K3 rnds.

With Black, K4 rnds.

With Light Cantaloupe, *K1, K2tog; rep from * to
   end of rnd.

K3 rnds.

With Black, K2tog until you have 5 sts on needle.

Work I-Cord (see p. 115) on these 5 sts until cord
   measures approx 16 in. or desired length. Cut
   yarn, leaving a long tail. Thread needle and pass
   yarn through sts on needle, fastening off tightly.
   Carefully thread needle down the center of the
   I-Cord, bringing the needle into the WS of the
   crown of the hat. Pull tightly and gather to make
   your I-Cord squiggle. Secure and weave in all
   loose ends.

GIANT BOBBLES (MAKE 4 IN BRIGHT YELLOW AND 1 IN BRIGHT RED)

With straight needles, CO 10 sts. Work Seed st for
   approx 10 rows or until the piece is the shape of
   a square. Cut yarn, leaving an 8- to 10-in. tail.
   Thread a tapestry needle with the tail and pass
   through the sts on the needle, then pass through
   sts on side of square, on the bottom of the
   square and, finally, on the 3rd side. Pull until the
   entire square turns into a small round bobble.

FINISHING

Fasten the yellow bobbles around the brim using the
   tails to secure on the WS of the brim. Fasten the
   Bright Red bobble to the tip of the I-Cord.

Brim

With cardboard, cut a circle that is 1 (2) in. deep
   and 10 in. in circumference. Line up the Seed st
   brim with the cardboard. Turn brim at Ridge Rnd

and sew together with cardboard liner in place. This will help keep your witch's hat brim sitting upright.

Optional: Fill the crown of the hat with polyester filling to help keep the hat upright and gorgeous.

Fizzle Ruffle Beanie

Ruffles are an easy way to make any hat a fancy hat. This luscious multi-colored beanie is perfect for play dates, parties, and more.

Sizing

Small (14-in. circumference)

Large (16-in. circumference)

Figures for larger size are given below in
parentheses. Where only one set of figures
appears, the directions apply to both sizes.

Yarn

DK Weight smooth yarn

DK Weight eyelash yarn

The hat shown is made with S.R. Kertzer Super 10
Cotton: 100% mercerized cotton, 4.4 oz. (125 g)/
250 yd. (228.6 m); S.R. Kertzer Super 10 Cotton
Multi: 100% mercerized cotton, 3.5 oz. (100 g)/
220 yd. (201 m); and Trendsetter Yarns Aura:
100% nylon, 1.75 oz. (50 g)/145 yd. (133 m).

Yardage

70 (80) yd. Super 10 Cotton Multi #0494 Orange

40 (50) yd. Super 10 Cotton #3525 Cornsilk

30 yd. Aura #5 Autumn Leaves

Materials

16-in. U.S. size 4 circular needle

Four U.S. size 4 double-pointed needles

Stitch marker

Tapestry needle

GAUGE

22 sts = 4 in. with Super 10 Cotton

SEED STITCH

Rnd 1: *K1, P1; rep from * to end of rnd.

All other rnds: K the P sts and P the K sts.

Directions

HAT BASE

With circ needles and Orange, CO 72 (80) sts.
Place a st marker on right needle and, beginning
Rnd 1, join CO sts together, making sure that sts
do not become twisted on needle.

Rnd 1: P.

Work Seed st for 3 (3½) in.

BO all sts kw. With the RS of the hat facing you, bend the ruffle down toward you and expose the join between the bottom of the ruffle and the top of the Orange Seed st. With Orange, pick up and K1 st in each "upward" loop at this join. There should be 72 (80) sts. K with Orange for 4 rnds.

Rep from * until you have made 3 (4) ruffles.

After picking up the final 72 (80) sts, begin the dec rnds, putting sts on dpns when necessary.

DECREASE ROUNDS

Dec Rnd 1: *K7 (8) K2tog; rep from * to end of rnd.

Dec Rnd 2: *K6 (7) K2tog; rep from * to end of rnd.

Continue in established pattern, knitting 1 less st between decs until you have 4–6 sts on the needle. Cut the yarn, leaving a 6-in. tail. Using a tapestry needle, thread the tail through the remaining sts on the needles. Pull the yarn, gathering the sts tightly together, then secure the tail on the WS of the beanie.

RUFFLE

*Cut Orange and attach Cornsilk.

Rnd 1: K1f&b into every st. There should be 144 (160) sts on the needle. Work Seed st for 4 rnds.

Cut Cornsilk and attach Autumn leaves. P1 rnd.

FINISHING

Weave in all loose ends. Make a Pom-Pom (see p. 116) using Orange, Cornsilk, and Autumn leaves. Attach it to the top of the hat.

Standard Yarn Weights

NUMBERED BALL	DESCRIPTION	STS/4 IN.	NEEDLE SIZE
1 SUPER FINE	Sock, baby, fingering	27–32	2.25–3.25 mm (U.S. 1–3)
2 FINE	Sport, baby	23–26	3.25–3.75 mm (U.S. 3–5)
3 LIGHT	DK, light worsted	21–24	3.75–4.5 mm (U.S. 5–7)
4 MEDIUM	Worsted, afghan, Aran	16–20	4.5–5.5 mm (U.S. 7–9)
5 BULKY	Chunky, craft, rug	12–15	5.5–8.0 mm (U.S. 9–11)
6 SUPER BULKY	Bulky, roving	6–11	8 mm and larger (U.S. 11 and larger)

Knitting Needle Sizes

MILLIMETER RANGE	U.S. SIZE RANGE
2.25 mm	1
2.75 mm	2
3.25 mm	3
3.5 mm	4
3.75 mm	5
4 mm	6
4.5 mm	7
5 mm	8
5.5 mm	9
6 mm	10
6.5 mm	10½
8 mm	11
9 mm	13
10 mm	15
12.75 mm	17
15 mm	19
19 mm	35
25 mm	50

Special Stitches

Here are the stitches I use to give my hats a little something extra special. Read through the instructions and step-by-step illustrations before you start knitting and you'll have no problem with any of the fun touches that make each hat unique.

Bobble (MB)

With desired color yarn, K1, P1, K1 in the next st to make 3 sts from 1. Turn and K3. Turn and K3, then lift the second and third sts over the first st on the right needle.

Cable Cast-On

Insert right needle between first 2 sts on left needle. Wrap yarn as if to knit. Draw yarn through to complete st and slip this new st onto left needle.

Duplicate Stitch

Thread a tapestry needle with the desired color yarn. Bring the needle through from the WS of the work to the base of the knit st you wish to cover with a duplicate st on the front side. Insert the needle directly under the base of the knit st that lies above the st you wish to cover. Bring the needle down and insert it at the base of the same knit st. Bring the tip of the needle out at the base of the next st you wish to cover and repeat this process until you have covered all the desired sts in the design.

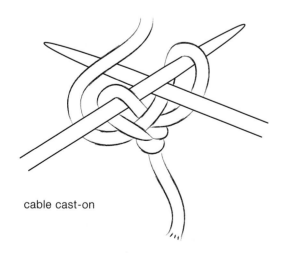

cable cast-on

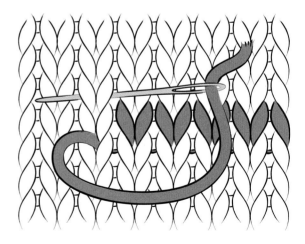

duplicate stitch

114

French Knot

Thread a tapestry needle with yarn and bring it from the WS of the work to the RS at the point where you wish to place the French Knot. Holding the yarn down with your left thumb, wind the yarn 3 times (for a small knot) or 4 to 6 times (for a large knot) around the needle. Still holding the yarn firmly, twist the needle back to the starting point and insert it close to where the yarn first emerged. Still holding the yarn down with your left thumb, slowly pull the yarn through to the WS to create a French Knot. Secure each knot on WS.

I-Cord

With two dpns, work I-Cord as follows: K4 to 6 sts. *Do not turn work. Slide sts to other end of needle, pull the yarn around the back, and knit the sts as usual. Repeat from * for desired length of cord.

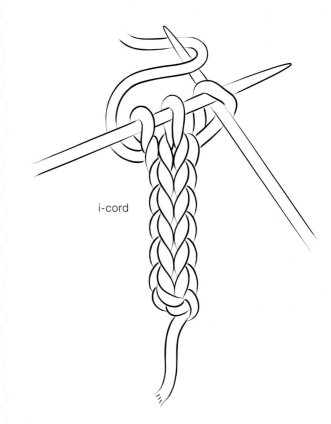

i-cord

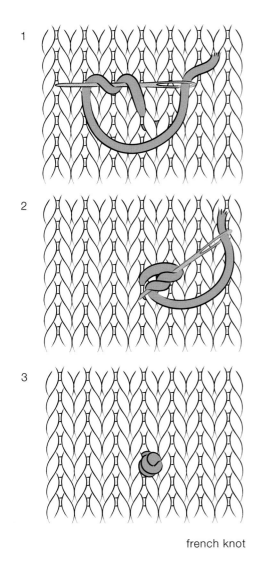

french knot

M1 Increase

With the left needle tip, lift the strand between the last st you have knitted and the next st on your left needle. Knit into the back of that st. One st has been made.

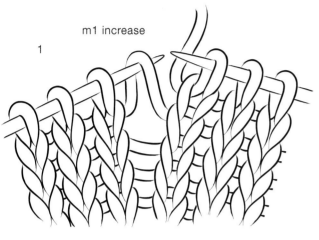

m1 increase

1

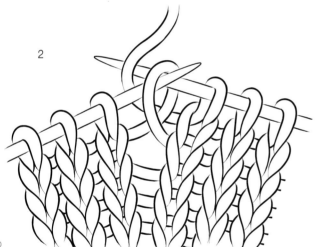

2

Pom-Pom

Many knitting books give directions that require the knitter to make a Pom-Pom maker, usually by cutting out a cardboard circle, figuring out the dimensions, and going from there. I have found that investing in an inexpensive Pom-Pom maker (the cost is usually less than $4.00) is the way to go. The one I like best is plastic and comes in several sizes, so I can make Pom-Poms that are very small or extra-large. For all the Pom-Poms in this book, I used a maker that had a 1$\frac{1}{2}$-in. to 2$\frac{1}{2}$-in. diameter. Always remember that the trick for a good, full Pom-Pom is to wrap the yarn around the maker as many times as possible. Your Pom-Pom will be full and stand proud!

Welt

Create a small welt by passing the needle over and under the pieces of knitting that you have "pinched" together, for example, at the side and crown of the hat. Weave both pieces (the side and crown) together using evenly spaced running sts that are approx $\frac{1}{4}$ in. from the crown edge. Sewing the two pieces together in this way will create a slight thickening or "welt" along the edge of the crown.

Abbreviations

approx	approximately
beg	beginning
BO	bind off
circ	circular
CO	cast on
cont	continue
dec	decrease/decreases/decreasing
dpn(s)	double-pointed needle(s)
inc	increase/increases/increasing
K	knit
K1f&b	knit in the front and in the back of the same stitch
K2tog	knit 2 stitches together
kw	knitwise
M1	make 1 stitch
MB	make bobble
P	Purl
psso	pass slipped stitch over
pw	purlwise
rem	remaining
rep	repeat
rnd	round
RS	right side
s2kp	slip 2 stitches together, knit 1, pass 2 slipped stitches over
skp	slip 1, knit 1, pass slipped stitch over knit 1
sl 1	slip 1 stitch
ssk	slip 1, slip 1, knit slipped stitches together
st(s)	stitch(es)
St st	stockinette stitch
tog	together
WS	wrong side
wyib	with yarn in back of work
yd	yard/yards
YO	yarn over

Metric Conversion Chart

One inch equals approximately 2.54 centimeters. To convert inches to centimeters, multiply the figure in inches by 2.54 and round off to the nearest half centimeter, or use the chart below, whose figures are rounded off (1 centimeter equals 10 millimeters).

⅛ in. = 3 mm	9 in. = 23 cm
¼ in. = 6 mm	10 in. = 25.5 cm
⅜ in. = 1 cm	12 in. = 30.5 cm
½ in. = 1.3 cm	14 in. = 35.5 cm
⅝ in. = 1.5 cm	15 in. = 38 cm
¾ in. = 2 cm	16 in. = 40.5 cm
⅞ in. = 2.2 cm	18 in. = 45.5 cm
1 in. = 2.5 cm	20 in. = 51 cm
2 in. = 5 cm	21 in. = 53.5 cm
3 in. = 7.5 cm	22 in. = 56 cm
4 in. = 10 cm	24 in. = 61 cm
5 in. = 12.5 cm	25 in. = 63.5 cm
6 in. = 15 cm	36 in. = 92 cm
7 in. = 18 cm	45 in. = 114.5 cm
8 in. = 20.5 cm	60 in. = 152 cm

Resources

DEBBY WARE KNITWARES

www.debbyware.com

LION BRAND YARN

34 West 15th Street

New York, NY 10011

www.lionbrand.com

MUENCH YARNS

1323 Scott Street

Petaluma, CA 94954

www.muenchyarns.com

SIRDAR SPINNING LTD.

Flanshaw Lane

Wakefield

West Yorkshire

WF2 9ND

United Kingdom

www.sirdar.co.uk

SKACEL COLLECTION, INC.

P.O. Box 88110

Seattle, WA 98138

www.skacelknitting.com

STYLECRAFT

P.O. Box 62

Keighley

West Yorkshire

BD21 1PP

United Kingdom

www.stylecraft-yarns.co.uk

TAHKI STACY CHARLES

70-60 83rd Street, Building #12

Glendale, NY 11385

www.tahkistacycharles.com

TRENDSETTER YARNS

16745 Saticoy Street

Van Nuys, CA 91406

www.trendsetteryarns.com

WESTMINSTER FIBERS

(distributor of S.R. Kertzer)

165 Ledge Street

Nashua, NH 03060

www.westminsterfibers.com

Index

About the Author

Debby Ware discovered knitting as a child, when her mother taught her the basics, and she has loved it ever since. After graduating from the School of Visual Arts in New York City, she worked for various freelance designers knitting swatches and sample sweaters.

She also loved to make one-of-a-kind sweaters for her family and friends. Eventually, she began her pattern and knitting kit business where she sells her designs to knitting shops all over the country and online at debbyware.com. She lives on Martha's Vineyard with her husband Will, Buster the Cat, and Bessie the Bassett Hound.

So far in her career she has not created one sweater for her son Owen. He doesn't like to wear sweaters.